African-American Principals

Recent Titles in
Contributions in Afro-American and African Studies

African-American Principals

School Leadership and Success

KOFI LOMOTEY

CONTRIBUTIONS IN AFRO-AMERICAN AND
AFRICAN STUDIES, NUMBER 124

GREENWOOD PRESS
New York • Westport, Connecticut • London

Library of Congress Cataloging-in-Publication Data

Lomotey, Kofi.
  African-American principals : school leadership and success / Kofi Lomotey.
    p. cm. — (Contributions in Afro-American and African
  studies, ISSN 0069-9624 ; no. 124.)
    Bibliography: p.
    Includes index.
    ISBN 0-313-26375-2 (alk. paper)
    1. Afro-American school principals. 2. School management and
  organization—United States. 3. School supervision—United States.
  4. Afro-American children—Education. 5. Academic achievement.
  I. Title. II. Series.
  LB2806.L58 1989
  371.2'012'08996073—dc19   89-1881

British Library Cataloguing in Publication Data is available.

Library of Congress Catalog Card Number: 89-1881
ISBN: 0-313-26375-2
ISSN: 0069-9624

First published in 1989

Greenwood Press, Inc.
88 Post Road West, Westport, Connecticut 06881

Printed in the United States of America

The paper used in this book complies with the
Permanent Paper Standard issued by the National
Information Standards Organization (Z39.48-1984).

10 9 8 7 6 5 4 3 2 1

Contents

Illustrations

Preface

For nearly twenty years I have been deeply concerned with the persistent and pervasive underachievement of African-American students in America's public schools. To attempt to explain the underlying reasons is overwhelming to say the least. The causes are numerous, including the quality of teachers, the adequacy of school resources, the socioeconomic status of the students, the cultural relevance of the curriculum, and the quality of school leadership. In this book I investigate the impact of school leadership—specifically the principal's leadership—on the academic achievement of African-American students.

This book will be useful to educational administration students. In it I consider the recent literature on instructional leadership (or instructional management) and offer a fresh definition of the concept. I then describe how the principals in a given sample demonstrate this configuration of instructional management. Educational administration students will also benefit from a discussion of three additional qualities which the principals in the sample held in common—compassion, commitment, and confidence.

The book will be of value in the increasing number of courses across the country focusing on urban schools. In addition, courses on school effectiveness and school leadership could benefit from using this volume. Programs in black studies could use the book as a text when considering African-American education. Because my study focuses on the impact of African-American principals on the academic achievement of African-American students, African-American educators—scholars and practitioners—provide an additional siginificant audience.

Moreover, I provide for the interested reader another approach to looking at the problem of the poor academic achievement of African-American students in America's public schools with a focus on the impact of the principal's leadership on school climate.

Perhaps most importantly, I have taken great pains to write a book that is readable not only by professional educators, but by parents, community people, and other laypeople. The interesting, informative data coupled with the easy reading style make the book desirable both inside and outside of the classroom.

Acknowledgments

The most promising research plans are useless without receptive respondents. The principals who were in my study were the epitome of receptiveness. I felt at home in each of the schools that I studied, and this was due in large part to the warmth displayed by the principals, their office staffs, and their teachers. I will forever be indebted to them. Unfortunately these individuals and their institutions must remain anonymous. I would like to thank them publicly for their support of my research and I also would like for others to know who these fine examples of African-American leadership are. I cannot do either.

I would also like to acknowledge Larry Cuban, Milbrey McLaughlin, Juanita McKinley, and Ed Bridges of Stanford University. I would also like to acknowledge my good friend, Peter Harris.

My wife, Nahuja, is a unique example of African-American womanhood. While completing this study was by no means easy, it would have been a much greater challenge without Nahuja by my side. It takes a unique woman to have done all that she has done and continues to do. Our relationship has grown stronger through this experience. For that I am thankful.

Certainly many others, including Mark Fetler in the California Department of Education, were helpful. My apologies to all whose names I have omitted. Be assured that I greatly appreciated their assistance.

African-American Principals

1

Introduction

Over the years a number of studies have shown principal leadership to be a significant factor in more successful schools[1] (Phi Delta Kappa, 1980; Edmonds and Frederiksen, 1978; Vallina, 1978; Venezsky and Winfield, 1980).[2] This research has identified several important aspects of principal leadership. Principal leadership reflecting friendship, trust, respect, and warmth in relations with teachers has been associated with improved academic achievement (Keeler and Andrews, 1963; McMahon-Dumas, 1981). Such congenial relations between principals and teachers appear to foster more positive interaction between teachers and students, bringing about improved student academic performance (Brookover and Lezotte, 1979; Rist, 1973). Instructional leadership or instructional management has been found to be linked to improved performance as well, though there have been slight variations in the definitions of these terms (Weber, 1971; New York State Department of Education, 1974; Venezsky and Winfield, 1979). Generally, these terms have been used to describe principal leadership that focuses on making sure that: (1) instruction is handled effectively through such techniques as classroom observation and teacher evaluation; (2) the curriculum is regularly reviewed and improved to maintain its appropriateness for the students; and (3) student achievement is closely monitored.

Up to now most research has looked at the relationship between principal leadership and academic achievement without considering the possible effects of the race of the principal. Specifically, no studies have explored the impact the race of the principal has on the academic achievement of African-American elementary school students. Also, there has been no research that has looked at the impact of the leadership of African-American principals on the academic performance of African-American students.

This gap in the research is significant because academic success continues to be an elusive goal for the majority of African-American students. Despite virtuous aims and copious oratory with regard to equal educational opportunity, America has frequently failed to educate African-American children effectively. In fact, the academic achievement of African-American children in public schools has always trailed far behind that of their white peers (Coleman et al., 1966; Jencks et al., 1972; Marcus and Stickney, 1981; Adler, 1984; Stickney and Plunkett, 1983; Rist, 1973).

Available, albeit limited, evidence suggests that African-American principals positively affect the academic achievement of African-American students and that African-American leaders—and African-American principals, in particular—lead differently than their white peers. It is possible, therefore, that a separate body of research on the relationship between African-American principal leadership and African-American student achievement could yield results that differ from those that have been obtained thus far in the general research.

Culture is important when looking at the significance of African-American principals' influence upon African-American students. African-Americans have a distinct culture. This view has been disputed in the literature, but is generally accepted at present (Blauner, 1972; Pinkney, 1976).[3] Culture can be defined by looking at seven components: mythology, ethos, creative motif, political organization, economic organization, social organization, and history (Karenga, 1980). Each ethnic group has these seven characteristics, and it is the uniqueness of each quality and the combination of these seven qualities in a given ethnic group that determines the way a group and the individuals within it relate to the world.

There is, however, another body of literature that suggests that race is becoming less important while class is becoming more important in the behavior of African-Americans and other ethnic groups (Wilson, 1980; Sowell, 1981).[4] While I acknowledge the impact of socioeconomic status on behavior, I contend that the culture of a people defines (1) situations, (2) attitudes, values, and goals, (3) myths, legends, and the supernatural, and (4) behavior patterns (Horton and Hunt, 1968). The way a person relates to others and to circumstances that he or she encounters is shaped by the culture of that individual; African-American people respond differently to situations than do people from other cultures in America. Consider, for example, an African-American principal about to discipline an African-American student. If we assume that race culture is more significant than class culture, the principal would, consciously or unconsciously, draw upon African-American cultural views with regard to discipline (i.e., the ways African-Americans, as a race, have historically looked upon and dealt with discipline). The principal would also consider the situation in a way that a nonAfrican-American might not be able, given his or her unique cultural basis for looking at the world. On the other hand, Sowell and others might argue that such a principal would be influenced by his or her socioeconomic status and respond in a certain way to a lower-class child.

Looking at the relationship between African-American principals and African-American students from another perspective, it has been acknowledged that effective communication or interaction comes about when two people are similar (MacLennan, 1975). This concept is known as homophily (Rogers and Shoemaker, 1971). People who have homogeneous beliefs, values, attributes, educational background, or social status tend to interact and communicate more effectively with each other (Kochman, 1981). When two African-Americans interact or communicate, their shared beliefs and values suggest that homophily

homophily occurs, bringing about greater information usage, attitude formation, attitude change, and behavior change. For example, homophily occurs in the communication and interaction between an African-American principal and African-American students, as a result of their cultural likeness. This may be a desirable situation since homophily may make interaction and the exchange of thoughts and messages more effective and beneficial to all involved, ultimately affecting academic achievement.

A brief look at the relationship between African-American teachers and African-American students is instructive. Research suggests that teacher race may have an impact on student achievement. A few researchers have found that African-American teachers can positively affect the achievement of African-American students (Murnane, 1975; Spady, 1973; Greenleigh Associates, 1966). In this research, the academic achievement scores of African-American students with African-American teachers and the scores of African-American students with white teachers were compared. The results of these studies showed that scores of the African-American students with African-American teachers were higher, suggesting that African-American students do better academically with teachers of their own racial background. One may infer from this that African-American principals might also have a positive effect on the academic achievement of African-American students.[5]

African-American and white leaders do appear to lead differently. In the area of education, African-American principals seem to place a higher priority on community involvement in the educational milieu than do their white colleagues (Monteiro, 1977). They are more inclined, as a group, to involve parents and other community members in school activities and, to a degree, in decision making. They view such involvement as fundamental to the overall success of the school and to their individual success. African-American principals may be less threatened by a focus on community relations, as they tend to relate more closely with the larger community. In African-

American schools it is possible that this emphasis on the larger community may be a key ingredient in bringing about improved academic performance for African-American students.[6] It is also possible that African-American principals are able to foster such a relationship (in a way that would elude principals of other races) because of the similarity of their attitudes, values, and goals to those of the larger African-American community.

One study suggests that African-Americans tend to be less expressive and more inhibited in the exercise of their leadership responsibilities (Allen, 1973). What may be a lack of confidence and a lack of comfort could cause these leaders to be less vocal and less directive. This tendency could also be attributed to their culture. It is possible that what may be construed as inhibition may be a culturally different way of dealing with leadership. This tendency may have an impact upon the relations that develop between African-American leaders and their subordinates, subsequently altering and distinguishing their leadership.

Because African-American leaders appear to be less expressive and more inhibited than other leaders, their subordinates could respond differently to them, creating a different supervisor/subordinate relationship. For example, teachers who are accustomed to working with a white principal, whom they think of as being more expressive, might not be as responsive to an African-American principal, whom they perceive as being less expressive. The principal might respond by altering his or her leadership style in order to bring about the desired response from the teachers.

Also, subordinates may react differently to their supervisor depending upon the supervisor's race (Parker, 1976). If subordinates react differently to supervisors based upon the supervisor's race, this could affect the leadership of the supervisor along racial lines, again differentiating the leadership of African-American and white leaders.

These school leadership studies and general leadership studies suggest that African-American principals may exercise leadership differently. Moreover, the race of the principal may affect African-American academic achievement, and African-American and white principals may lead differently. While one might assume that African-American principals are instructional managers in more successful schools, it may be that, in African-American schools with African-American principals, instructional management encompasses something other than teacher supervision and evaluation, curriculum planning, and evaluation of achievement. Perhaps instructional management for African-American principals is personified in getting parents and other community members involved in the school instead of (or in addition to) the above manifestations. At present, it cannot be said that what is known about principal leadership is necessarily applicable to African-American principals.

The research suggesting differences in the African-American principal–predominantly African-American school relationship, linked with the questionable applicability of research on principal leadership, provide the rationale for the racial distinction employed in this book. Generally, my intent was to explore whether African-American principals in more successful African-American schools possess the qualities suggested by the research on principal leadership and academic achievement.

It is the insufficient understanding of the relationship between African-American principal leadership and African-American academic achievement in African-American elementary schools that motivated this research and framed my central research problem. This book is exploratory in nature and consists of three case studies. It focuses on developing an understanding of the leadership of African-American principals in African-American schools. I begin by posing the general question: what kind of leadership do African-American principals exhibit in more successful African-American elementary schools?

NOTES

1. I define "more successful schools" as schools that appear in the upper third of a rank ordering of the population of predominantly African-

American elementary schools in California. The rank ordering is based upon a composite score for each school of the third- and sixth-grade math and reading scale scores on the California Assessment Program (CAP) Test for the years 1980–81 and 1981–82.

2. The principal has also been found to be of paramount importance in bringing about change in schools, according to the school improvement literature (Clark, Lotto, and Astuto, 1984; Berman and McLaughlin, 1975; Fullan, 1982).

3. The opponents of this view argue that the elimination of African cultural heritage brought about a total acculturation of African-Americans and that their culture is therefore influenced solely by the American culture (Myrdal, 1944; Glazer and Moynihan, 1973; Frazier, 1957; Banfield, 1970). Herskovits, a cultural anthropologist, and others have long acknowledged an African-American culture, arguing that there are African-American ethnic patterns that are African (Herskovits, 1941; Sarason, 1976; Havighurst, 1976).

While I do not believe that the culture of African-Americans is identical to that in any part of Africa, I do hold that African-Americans have combined their African heritage with the American experience to create a unique culture, much in the same way that other ethnic groups in America have developed their own distinguishable cultures. An appreciation for this duality in African-American culture is acknowledged by many social scientists, including DuBois (DuBois, 1961).

4. Scholars who support this contention argue that while race is important in America, a monolithic view of the African-American presence in America obscures the significant differences in experiences obtained by the various classes of African-Americans (Wilson, 1980; Sowell, 1981).

In fact, as early as 1947, Davis and Havighurst conducted a study in which they interviewed African-American and white, lower- and middle-class mothers and concluded that class differences are more significant than color differences in the development of one's personality.

While I acknowledge that all groups have class cultures as well as a race culture (Havighurst, 1976; Hale, 1982), my view, like that of Karenga and others, is that the impact of the race culture predominates (Karenga, 1978; Hale, 1982; Stodolsky and Lesser, 1967).

5. This logic assumes that principals influence teachers, who, in turn, influence students to create more successful schools. This line of

reasoning is supported in the effective schools' literature (Brookover and Lezotte, 1979; Rist, 1973).

6. I define "African-American schools" as elementary schools that have a student population that is two-thirds or more African-American.

REFERENCES

Adler, S., ed. 1984. *Cultural Language Differences*. Springfield. Ill: Charles C. Thomas.

Allen, G. R. 1973. *The Graduate Students' Guide to Theses and Dissertations*. San Francisco: Jossey-Bass.

Banfield, E. 1970. *The Unheavenly City*. Boston: Little, Brown.

Berman, P., and M. W. McLaughlin. 1975. *Federal Programs Supporting Educational Change: The Process of Change*. Santa Monica, Calif: Rand.

Blauner, R. 1972. *Racial Oppression in America*. New York: Harper and Row.

Brookover, W., and L. W. Lezotte. 1979. "Changes in school characteristics coincident with changes in student achievement." East Lansing: Michigan State University, College of Urban Development.

Clark, D. L., L. S. Lotto, T. A. Astuto. 1985. "Effective schools and school improvement: A comparative analysis of two lines of inquiry." *Educational Administration Quarterly* 20, no. 3: 41–68.

Coleman, J. S., et al. 1966. *Equality of Educational Opportunity*. Washington, D.C.: U.S. Government Printing Office.

Davis, W. A., and R. J. Havighurst. 1947. *Father of the Man*. Boston: Houghton Mifflin.

DuBois, W. E. B. 1961. *The Souls of Black Folk: Essays and Sketches*. Greenwich, Conn.: Fawcett.

Edmonds, R., and J. R. Frederiksen. 1978. *Search for Effective Schools: The Identification and Analysis of City Schools That Are Instructionally Effective for Poor Children*. Cambridge: Harvard University Center for Urban Studies.

Frazier, E. F. 1957. *The Negro in the United States*. New York: Macmillan.

Fullan, M. 1982. *The Meaning of Educational Change*. New York: Teachers' College Press, Teachers' College, Columbia University.

Glazer, N., and D. P. Moynihan. 1973. *Beyond the Melting Pot: The Negroes, Puerto Ricans, Jews, Italians and Irish in New York City*. Cambridge, Mass.: Harvard University Press.

Greenleigh Associates. 1966. *Field Test and Evaluation of Selected Adult Basic Education Systems.* New York: Greenleigh Associates.

Hale, J. 1982. *Black Children: Their Roots, Culture, and Learning Styles.* Provo, Utah: Brigham Young University Press.

Havighurst, R. J. 1976. "The relative importance of social class and ethnicity in human development." *Human Development* 19, no. 1: 56–64.

Herskovits, M. 1941. *The Myth of the Negro Past.* New York: Harper and Row.

Horton, P., and C. Hunt. 1968. *Sociology.* 2d ed. New York: McGraw-Hill.

Jencks, C., et al. 1972. *Inequality: A Reassessment of the Effects of Family and Schooling in America.* New York: Basic Books.

Karenga, M. 1978. *Essays on Struggle: Position and Analysis.* San Diego: Kawaida.

————. 1980. *Kawaida Theory: An Introductory Outline.* Englewood, Calif.: Kawaida.

Keeler, B. T. and Andrews, J. H. M. 1963. "The behavior of principals: Staff morale and productivity." *Alberta Journal of Educational Research* 9 (September 1963), 179–91.

Kochman, T. 1981. *Black and White Styles in Conflict.* Chicago: University of Chicago Press.

MacLennan, B. W. 1975. "The personalities of group leaders: Implications for selecting and training." *International Journal of Group Psychotherapy* 25, no. 2: 177–83.

Marcus, L. R., and B. D. Stickney. 1981. *Race and Education: The Unending Controversy.* Springfield, Ill.: Charles C. Thomas.

McMahon-Dumas, C. E. 1981. "An investigation of the leadership styles and effectiveness dimensions of principals, and their relationship with reading gain scores of students in the Washington DC public schools," Ed. D. diss., George Washington University.

Monteiro, T. 1977. "Ethnicity and the perceptions of principals." *Integrated Education* 15, no. 3: 15–16.

Murnane, R. J. 1975. *The Impact of School Resources on the Learning of Inner City Children.* Cambridge, Mass.: Ballinger.

Myrdal, G. 1944. *An American Dilemma: The Negro Problem and Modern Democracy.* New York: Harper.

New York State Department of Education. 1974. "School factors influencing reading achievement: A case study of two inner city schools." Albany, N.Y.: Office of Education Performance Review.

Parker, W. S., Jr. 1976. "Black-white differences in leadership behavior related to subordinates' reactions." *Journal of Applied Psychology* 61, no. 2: 140–47.

Phi Delta Kappa. 1980. *Why Do Some Urban Schools Succeed? The Phi Delta Kappan Study of Exceptional Urban Elementary Schools.* Bloomington, Ind.: Phi Delta Kappa.

Pinkney, A. 1976. *Red, Black and Green.* New York: Cambridge University Press.

Rist, R. 1973. *The Urban School: A Factory of Failure.* Cambridge, Mass.: MIT.

Rogers, E. M., and F. F. Shoemaker. 1971. *Communication of Innovation: A Cross-Cultural Approach.* New York: Free Press.

Sarason, S. 1976. "Jewishness, blackishness and the nature-nurture controversy." *American Psychologist* 28, no. 11: 962–71.

Sowell, T. 1981. *Ethnic America: A History.* New York: Basic.

Spady, W. 1973. "The impact of school resources on students." In *Review of Research in Education—I*, ed. F. N. Kerlinger, 135–77. Itasca, Ill.: F. E. Peacock.

Stickney, B. D., and V. R. L. Plunkett. 1983. "Closing the gap: A historical perspective on the effectiveness of compensatory education." *Phi Delta Kappan* 65, no. 4: 287–90.

Stodolsky, S. S., and G. S. Lesser. 1967. "Learning patterns in the disadvantaged." *Harvard Educational Review* 37, no. 4: 546–93.

Vallina, S. A. 1978. "Analysis of observed critical task performance of title I—ESEA principals, state of Illinois." Ed. D. diss., University of Chicago.

Venezsky, R. L., and L. Winfield. 1979. "Schools that succeed beyond expectations in teaching reading." Newark, Del.: University of Delaware Studies on Education, Technical Report No. 1.

Weber, G. 1971. *Inner City Children Can Be Taught to Read: Four Successful Schools.* Washington, D.C.: Council for Basic Education.

Wilson, W. J. 1980. *The Declining Significance of Race: Blacks and Changing American Institutions.* Chicago: University of Chicago Press.

2

Previous Research on the Principal's Influence on Academic Achievement

INTRODUCTION

I reviewed twenty-nine studies that address the relationship between the elementary school principal's leadership and academic achievement (see table 2.1).[1] Fifteen studies relied primarily on observational data. Effectiveness (or success) was defined in each of these studies in terms of academic achievement. Most studies use a composite of math and reading achievement scores or reading scores only (see table 2.1). In an attempt to synthesize the literature, I developed a framework drawn from existing studies for this review (see figure 2.1). This framework provides the basis for the following discussion.[2]

QUALITATIVE STUDIES

Barsky (1975), in a case study of one urban school principal in Pennsylvania, asked two questions: What is the leadership style of this principal in a successful urban school? What impact has this principal made on the education of his students? Barksy began with the assumption that the role of the principal is important

Table 2.1
Overview of Reviewed Studies

Author(s)	Sample Size	Instruments	Ach't Measure
Armor et al. (1970)	20	inter., quest.	reading
Austin (1979)	30	questionnaires	composite
Barsky (1975)	1	obser., quest., doc.	composite
Brookover et al. (1979)	150	questionnaires	reading and math
Brookover and Lezotte (1979)	8	inter., quest.	composite
CA State Dept. of Ed. (1977)	42	quest., inter., obser.	composite
Clancy (1982)	19	doc., inter., symp.	composite
Coulson (1977)	50	obser., inter.	composite
DeGuire (1980)	10	quest., obser.	reading
Doll (1967)	40	obser., inter.	composite
Edmonds and Frederiksen (1979)	4	questionnaires	reading
Felsenthal (1982)	1	inter., obser.	nat'l recognition
Gervais (1982)	6	observation	reading
Glenn (1981)	4	observations	reading and math
Jackson, Logsdon, and Taylor (1983)	8	quest., inter.	CTBS
Jun (1981)	280	questionnaires	composite
Kean et al. (1979)	25	interviews	reading scores
Levine and Stark (1981)	9	interviews	reading scores
Marcus et al. (1976)	24	inter., quest., obser.	math scores
McMahon-Dumas (1981)	not provided	questionnaires	reading scores
Moody and Amos (1975)	1	(not provided)	reading and math
NYS Office of Ed. (1974)	1	inter., obser.	reading scores
Phi Delta Kappa (1980)	8	obser., inter., quest.	composite score

Table 2.1 (continued)

Author(s)	Sample Size	Instruments	Ach't Measure
Vallina (1978)	20	observations	reading
Venezsky and Winfield (1980)	2	inter., obser., doc.	reading scores
Weber (1971)	4	obser., inter.	reading scores
Wellisch et al. (1977)	26	quest., inter., obser.	CAT scores
Wilson (1982)	1	obser., inter.	(not provided)
Wolfson (1980)	25	questionnaires	reading scores

in the educational process. The variables studies included manipulation of rewards, attention to detail, sense of loyalty, sense of self-efficacy, and emphasis on the human factor within the organizational role. Barsky's findings indicated that this principal's style resembled that of a traditional ward leader. Observer bias may have been generated in the study, however, due to the researcher's personal relationship with the principal.

The California State Department of Education (1977) studied the educational factors that produce the differences in student achievement. The goal was to distinguish the effects of educational and environmental factors that have an impact on student achievement. Variables considered included staff

Figure 2.1
Framework for Examining the Research on Principal Leadership and Academic Achievement
(with a Focus on Principal/Teacher Relations)

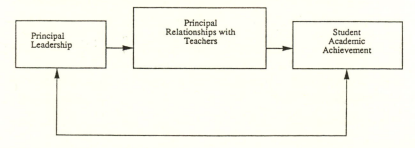

characteristics, student/staff contact, and organizational processes. The researchers studied twenty-one pairs of high performing and low performing schools focusing on the sixth-grade classes. They concluded that staff level of satisfaction with administrators is important and that schools should consider the importance of training teachers to monitor student learning and progress. The study was limited in that it was only the first phase of a larger study; there remained a need to consider several puzzling findings. For example, results indicated that children in the *low* achieving schools received more instruction in mathematics.

P. L. Clancy (1982) conducted a study in which he explored the question of what qualities characterize an effective school. Nineteen schools in seventeen districts in Michigan participated in the study. Seven key characteristics were:

- high degree of staff intercommunication
- mastery learning emphasized in instructional program
- strong principal leadership
- stable, flexible, innovative, and skilled staff
- supportive parents
- a superintendent who clearly communicates the importance of academic achievement
- clear expectations of teachers, administrators, and students

Focusing on the role of the principal in a school's reading program, M. R. DeGuire (1980) investigated how the principal influences reading achievement. Variables considered included goal and program development, program coordination and delivery, supervision and evaluation, staff development, community relations, knowledge, and attitude. The sample included ten elementary schools in Colorado—five effective and five ineffective. DeGuire concluded that the following were key factors in effective schools: the principal's awareness of responsibility for instructional leadership of the school's reading program; clear and consistent procedures in providing reading materials;

and effective communication with parents and the larger community.

R. Edmonds and J. R. Frederiksen (1978) studied two urban schools in Detroit—one effective and one ineffective. They asked the question: What are the characteristics of schools that are instructionally effective for poor children? They concluded that all children are educable and that the behavior of the school principal is the most crucial factor in effective schools.

In attempting to identify and define the factors that are related to school effectiveness, H. Felsenthal (1982) focused on six variables: leadership, expectations, instruction, climate, evaluation, and parental involvement. She studied one elementary school in an eastern urban community. She concluded that strong principal leadership is the most crucial factor in effective schools.

In a similar study, B. C. Glenn (1981) sought to identify the factors that cause schools to be effective educators for poor African-American children. Factors explored included goals of achievement, instruction, leadership, and climate. Four schools located in Richmond, Virginia, Baltimore, Maryland, and New York, New York, served as the sample. The most significant finding was that improvement of the professional skills and characteristics of the staff in schools is most important in making schools effective for poor children. A wide-ranging literature review accompanied the study.

In comparing four effective and four ineffective predominantly African-American schools in Washington, D.C., S. A. Jackson, D. M. Logsdon, and N. E. Taylor (1983) considered the leadership behaviors that distinguish effective, low-income urban schools from ineffective schools. Behaviors which they explored fit into four categories: school goals and standards, positive school climate and expectations for success, curriculum and instruction emphasizing basic skills and coordination linkages, and parent/community support. They concluded that it is important for the principal to be a powerful taskmaster and supporter of teachers and students. Notably, the researchers describe in detail the leadership behaviors that are significant for principals in effective schools.

A. C. Marcus et al. (1976) conducted an observational study with a sample of twenty-four schools. The intent was to explore the relationship between principal leadership and student achievement. Significant among the findings was that schools where principals are involved in instructional and curricular decision making are more likely to show increases in math and reading achievement.

In a study by the New York State Office of Education (1974), the researchers sought to determine what distinguishes effective schools from ineffective schools. They examined one high achieving school and one low achieving school in New York, New York. Characteristics that they focused on included administrative characteristics, teacher characteristics, reading methods, and classroom, school, and community climates. They concluded that school factors are more important than nonschool factors in bringing about student achievement.

In a two-part study, researchers for Phi Delta Kappa (1980) began by looking at eight elementary schools in several states and attempted to determine how effective schools become effective. Understanding the development of these schools is more important, the authors argue, than merely describing their characteristics. Findings showed that principal leadership was critical, a focus on reading and math was important, parent involvement was key, and the school's climate was a critical factor.

The second part of the study focused on a synthesis of several other studies. In this review, three areas stood out as those requiring a concerted effort in bringing about effective schools: leadership, teachers, and curriculum and instruction. These factors, the researchers found, are interdependent and must be conceptualized and considered accordingly.

By focusing on the process of success rather than the success itself and by reviewing a large number of studies (768) the study provides concrete and useful suggestions for those interested in improving urban schools.

R. L. Venezsky and L. Winfield (1979) focus on factors associated with schools in the Atlantic coastal area that are effective in teaching reading to low socioeconomic status elementary school students. They concentrated on two sets of variables, leadership and instruction. They conclude that the emphasis in reading instruction should be shifted away from instructional methods and teacher accountability to the principal's role and the efficiency of the school's instructional program. Overall, this study is somewhat poorly organized and the description of the sample unclear.

G. Weber (1971) concentrated on identifying the factors contributing to the success of good reading programs in urban public schools. He explored four successful urban schools in New York City, Kansas City, and Los Angeles, focusing on the third grade. The criteria for success was reading achievement. A major conclusion of the study was that successful reading programs are the result of efforts on the part of the school and are less reliant on student characteristics.

Twenty-two schools—nine effective and thirteen ineffective—were the focus of a study by J. B. Wellisch et al. (1977). The question guiding the research was: What characterizes the management and organization of schools that are effective in raising student achievement? Variables included academic standards, coordination of the instructional program, and three dimensions of administrative leadership (concern, communication, and responsibility for instruction). The researchers concluded that schools with principals who employ a general intervention strategy facilitating a coordinated schoolwide program are most successful. Moreover, the researchers agreed that the capabilities of staff must be supported and developed.

K. Wilson (1982) attempted to delineate the qualities of an effective principal. He concludes, in his case study of one school in Massachusetts, that a commitment on the part of the principal to the instructional process is an important quality of principals in effective schools.

QUANTITATIVE STUDIES

D. Armor et al. (1976) investigated school and classroom policies and other factors that are most successful in raising the reading scores of children in urban schools. Variables included school leadership, reading program content and implementation, classroom atmosphere, and teacher attributes. Twenty Los Angeles elementary schools were studied. The researchers concluded that reading program policies, teacher involvement in program planning, and allocation of decision-making authority to schools and teachers are important components of programs aiming to increase the reading achievement of students in urban schools.

G. R. Austin (1979) reviewed several studies in which researchers were investigating factors that make an effective school different. He concluded that in order for a school to be effective, personnel and parents must agree on goals. Moreover, in such schools, teachers must be stimulated and given freedom from administrative intervention so that they can feel that the effort to increase student achievement is worthwhile.

W. Brookover et al. (1979) posited that student achievement is affected by the social system. Variables they considered were social input, social structure, and social climate. They concluded that effective schools are characterized by high evaluations of students, high expectations, and high norms of achievement.

Brookover and Lezotte (1979) looked at eight Michigan elementary schools—six improving and two declining—to determine what changes in schools coincided with the improvement or decline in student achievement. Six classes of variables were explored: school organization functions, methods and materials, policies and practices, interpersonal relationships, staff perceptions of the students, and community and staff perceptions of effectiveness. The researchers concluded that mastery of the basic skills by all students, common academic expectations for all students, and the principal's leadership in the school's instructional program should be emphasized. A strength of the study was the uniqueness of the research design—looking at the changes rather than the key characteristics in effective schools.

J. E. Coulson (1977) sought to identify key characteristics of effective schools. With a large national sample he conducted a preliminary survey and followed up with an in-depth observational study. Principal leadership was shown to be a major factor in a school's ability to improve student achievement.

In a study conducted through the University of Missouri Research Center for the Study of Metropolitan Problems in Education, R. C. Doll (1967) sought to determine factors associated with school success. Prominent among the findings were that the principal's leadership was the key factor and that the way that schools were grouped (K-6 rather than K-8 was preferable) also had an effect on academic achievement.

R. L. Gervais (1982) conducted a study in which he explored the possible effect a principal may have on the reading achievement of children in a classroom. The study included six schools—three for experimental purposes and three as a control group. The three experimental schools (which consciously tried to boost reading achievement) reported unusually high scores after the treatment. Gervais concluded that though different methods were used in each of the three schools, the fact that the principal showed support for teachers and students was of paramount importance.

S. Jun (1981) investigated the relationship between student achievement, principal leadership, and teacher job satisfaction. Two hundred eighty principals, 903 fourth-grade teachers, and students from 280 schools in Korea were included in the study. There was no conclusive evidence that teacher attitude affected student achievement. The most significant finding was that 54 percent of the variance in student achievement was explained by the principals' leadership.

In a quantitative study, M. H. Kean et al. (1979) sought to identify critical factors in schools that bring about high reading achievement for students. Eighteen hundred Philadelphia fourth-grade students made up the sample. Four key factors identified in the study were: (1) use of a linguistic basal approach to reading instruction; (2) having former reading professionals as principals; (3) more time on task by teachers; and (4) a combination of whole class and small group instruction.

D. U. Levine and J. Stark (1981) examined nine schools in Chicago, New York, and Los Angeles. Several findings emerged from the study. Most notable was that outstanding administrative leadership was key. Such leaders were defined as those who are supportive of teachers, skilled in instructional matters, and willing to interpret rules with an eye toward program effectiveness.

C. E. McMahon-Dumas (1981) studied the relationship between student reading achievement and task behavior and relationship behavior of principals in Washington, D.C., public schools. Through the use of a questionnaire, responses from the principals were collected and statistically analyzed. McMahon-Dumas concluded, most significantly, that high relationship behavior by the principal contributed most to high student achievement in reading.

In a study of the effect of principal leadership on student academic achievement, L. Moody and N. E. Amos (1975) concluded that if principals are involved in instructional planning with teachers, student academic achievement is likely to improve. These conclusions were based on a longtitudinal study of one school in which achievement scores had risen over two years in the presence of a principal. The principal left for one year and returned for the fourth year. The achievement level remained constant in the third year and rose again in the fourth year.

S. A. Vallina (1978) investigated how the leadership role in critical task areas (i.e. instruction, pupil personnel, community relations, staff personnel, and school plant/finances) compare for principals in successful and unsuccessful Title I elementary schools in Chicago. Ten successful and ten unsuccessful schools were selected for the study based upon academic achievement scores. The principals in the successful schools scored significantly higher in most of the areas.

A study by E. Wolfson (1980) explored two questions: What is the relationship between the leadership styles of elementary school principals and student reading achievement? How does student reading achievement vary based upon leadership style?

The sample included twenty-five principals in suburban New York City. The principal leadership variables, measured by a questionnaire, were high consideration–high initiating structure; high consideration–low initiating structure; low consideration–low initiating structure; and low consideration–high initiating structure.

Through the use of analyses of variance, it was found that there was no significant difference between the effects of the varying leadership styles on student achievement in reading. The author notes that the small number of principals in the study may have limited his ability to make adequate distinctions between leadership styles.

SUMMARY

The following findings were derived from this review of the literature:

First, principals in more successful schools are instructional managers and not just bureaucratic administrators (Wilson, 1982; DeGuire, 1980). While researchers offer various definitions for instructional management, regular involvement in curriculum planning, teacher supervision, and evaluation of academic achievement appear most often as manifestations (see table 2.2 for a summary of the various definitions of instructional management).

Second, principals in more successful schools are assertive (California State Department of Education, 1977; Venezsky and Winfield, 1980). They take responsibility for decision making and are active participants in the daily activities in their schools. Things that need to be done are done, and there is sufficient follow-through to allow for the smooth operation of all facets of the school.

Third, communication is important for principals in more effective schools (Coulson, 1977; Wellisch et al., 1978). The ability to effectively transmit information to teachers, and to receive information from teachers, is of significance to principals in

Table 2.2
How Previous Researchers Have Defined Instructional Management

	Regular Ach'm't Evaluation	Sets Up Improv. Program	Assertive Instruct. Leader	Regular Involvement in Curr. Planning	Regular Involvement in Curr. Dec. Making	Participation in Class	Regular Classroom Observation
SURVEY STUDIES							
Moody				X			
Marcus et al	X				X		
J.L. & T	X				X		
Edmonds et al.							X
Coulson				X			
CDSE							
B. & L.	X		X				
Austin			X		X	X	
Armor et al.							
Clancy							X
Wellisch et al.							X
CASE STUDIES							
Felsenthal	X						
DeGuire	X						
NYSOE		X		X			
Vallina							X
Venezsky & W.	X			X			
Weber	X			X			
Wilson							X

the daily management of their schools. There is less room for divergence from the collective goals of the school when lines of communication are open. This enables principals to articulate the goals to their staffs and allows staffs to solicit clarification of the school's direction. Also, principals involving teachers, where practical, in decision making at the school level is important for school success (New York State Office of Education, 1974; Glenn, 1981). This involvement aids in motivating staff to follow through on decisions. For example, teachers tend to feel an affinity for a curriculum that is collectively developed and, as a result, they are likely to utilize it more enthusiastically and effectively.

Fourth, support for staff is an important activity for principals in more successful schools (Brookover et al., 1979; Gervais, 1982). This support includes providing teachers with ample materials, participating in discussions with parents, being understanding of teachers' personal needs, and minimizing the amount of paper work required of teachers.

Finally, the behavior of principals in more effective schools is highly structured (Phi Delta Kappa, 1980; Edmonds and Frederiksen, 1978). These leaders follow a routine each day. They have appropriate, efficient forms for such activities as classroom observations and teacher evaluations and they are constantly aware of what is happening in each facet of the operation of their schools.

Although none of the above research focuses specifically on African-American principals, it does provide a basis for looking at the leadership of African-American principals in African-American schools; the review identifies one specific quality of principal leadership that seems to be important in most successful schools—instructional management. The relevant research questions are now stated in the following manner: (1) How do African-American principals in more successful African-American elementary schools demonstrate instructional management (i.e., a regular involvement in (a) the supervision and evaluation of teachers; (b) evaluation of academic achievement; and (c) curriculum planning) in their schools? (2)

Table 2.3
Principal Leadership and Relationships with Teachers

Author(s)	Assertive	Structured	Basic Skills Emph.	Task-oriented	Visible	Clear Goals	Communication	Supportive	Instruct. Leader	Coll. Decision Mkg.	Teacher Autonomy	Staff Development	Hires Staff
	Leadership						Relations with Teachers						
Armor et al (1976)	X									X			
Austin (1979)	X								X				
Barsky (1975)	X						X	X					
Brookover et al (1979)													
CA State Dept. of Ed. (1979)	X								X				
Coulson (1977)							X	X					
DeGuire (1980)								X					
Doll (1967)	X									X			
Edmonds and Frederiksen (1979)	X	X											
Felsenthal (1982)	X												
Glenn (1981)					X				X				
Jackson, Logsdon and Taylor (1983)	X			X	X								
Gervais (1982)								X					
Jun (1981)							X						
Kean et al (1979)									X				
Levine and Stark (1981)		X					X						
Marcus et al (1976)	X						X	X					
McMahon-Dumas (1981)													
Moody and Amos (1981)									X				
NYS Office of Education (1974)	X											X	
Phi Delta Kappan (1980)		X			X								
Vallina (1978)												X	X
Venezsky and Winfield (1980)	X											X	X
Weber (1971)												X	X
Wellisch et al (1977)	X								X	X			
Wilson (1982)	X											X	X
Wolfson (1980)													

What other leadership qualities, if any, do African-American principals in more successful African-American elementary schools hold in common?

NOTES

1. I limited my search to elementary schools because available research indicates that the behavior of the elementary school principal differs markedly from that of secondary school colleagues (Leithwood and Montgomery, 1982; Martinko and Gardner, 1983. I would like to acknowledge the examplary and extensive research assistance of Junko Kanamura, a graduate student in the Educational Organization, Administration and Policy Department at SUNY at Buffalo.

2. In my inquiry I concentrated on the relationship between the principal and teachers (see table 2.3 for a synopsis of this relationship.) I chose this focus because there is a substantial body of literature on principal leadership and academic achievement which suggests that the relationship between teachers and principals is of paramount importance (Brookover and Lezotte, 1977; Rist, 1973). Though there is some evidence to suggest that African-American principals are likely to focus on parental involvement, that literature is very limited. However, I do not intend to suggest that the relationships between the principal and the students, the school district, parents, and other community members do not affect the success of the school. Rather, my intent was to limit the focus of my exploratory inquiry. Where the effects of these other relationships are observed in this study, they are noted.

REFERENCES

Armor, D., et al. 1976. Analysis of the school preferred reading program in selected Los Angeles minority schools. Unpublished document. Santa Monica, Calif.: Rand.

Austin, G. R. 1979. "Exemplary schools and the search for effectiveness."*Educational Leadership* 37, no. 1: 10–14.

Barsky, H. 1975. "The political style of an urban principal: A case study." Ed. D. diss., University of Pennsylvania.

Brookover, W., et al. 1979. *School Social Systems and Student Achievement: Schools Can Make a Difference.* New York: Praeger.

Brookover, W., and L. Lezotte. 1979. *Changes in School Characteristics Concident with Changes in Student Achievement.* East Lansing: Michigan State University, College of Urban Development.

California State Department of Education. 1977. 1977 California School Effectiveness Study. The First Year: 1974–75. Sacramento, Calif.: Office of Program Evaluation and Research.

Clancy, P. L. 1982. *Nineteen Improving Schools and Why: Their Formula for Success.* Ypsilanti: Eastern Michigan University.

Coulson, J. E. 1977. *Overview of the National Evaluation of the Emerging School Aid Act.* Santa Monica, Calif.: System Development Corporation.

DeGuire, M. R. 1980. "The role of the elementary principal in influencing reading achievement." Ph.D. diss., University of Colorado.

Doll, R. C. 1967. *Variations among Inner City Elementary Schools: An Investigation into the Nature and Causes of the Differences.* Columbia, Mo.: University of Missouri Research Center for the Study of Metropolitan Problems in Education.

Edmonds, R., and J. R. Frederiksen. 1978. *Search for Effective Schools: The Identification and Analysis of City Schools That Are Instructionally Effective for Poor Children.* Cambridge: Harvard University, Center for Urban Studies.

Felsenthal, H. 1982. "Factors influencing school effectiveness: An ecological analysis of an effective school." Paper presented at the annual meeting of the American Educational Research Association, New York.

Gervais, R. L. 1982. "How do principals affect reading achievement?" *PTA Today* 7 (February): 25.

Glenn, B. C. 1981. *What Works? An Examination of Effective Schools for Poor Black Children.* Cambridge, Mass.: Harvard University Center for Law and Education.

Jackson, S. A., D. M. Lodsdon, and N. E. Taylor. 1983. "Instructional leadership behaviors: Differentiating effective from ineffective low-income urban schools." *Urban Education* 18, no. 1: 59–70.

Jun, S. 1981. "Principal leadership, teacher job satisfaction and student achievement in selected Korean elementary schools." Ph.D. diss., Florida State University.

Kean, M. H., et al. 1979. "What works in reading? The results of a joint school district federal reserve bank empirical study in Philadelphia." Office of Research and Evaluation.

Leithwood, K. A., and D. J. Montgomery. 1982. "The role of the elementary school principal in program development." *Review of Educational Research* 52, no. 3: 309–39.

Levine, D. U., and J. Stark. 1981. *Extended Summary and Conclusion: Instructional and Organizational Arrangements and Processes for Improving Academic Achievement at Inner City Elementary schools.* Kansas City, Mo.: University of Missouri, Kansas City School of Education Center for the Study of Metropolitan Problems in Education.

Marcus, A. C., et al. 1976. *Administrative Leadership in a Sample of Successful Schools from the National Evaluation of the Emergency School Aid Act.* Santa Monica, Calif.: System Development Corporation.

Martinko, W., and W. Gardner. 1983. *The Behavior of High Performing Educational Managers: An Observational Study.* Tallahassee: Florida State University.

McMahon-Dumas, C. E. 1981. "An investigation of the leadership styles of effectiveness dimensions of principals and their relationship with reading gain scores of students in the Washington DC public schools." Ed.D. diss., George Washington University.

Moody, L., and N. E. Amos. 1975. *The Impact of Principal Involvement in Instructional Planning with Teacher Teams on Academic Achievement of Elementary School Pupils.* Mississippi Bureau of Educational Research, Mississippi State University.

New York State Office of Education. 1974. *School Factors Influencing Reading Achievement: A Case Study of Two Inner City Schools.* Albany, N.Y.: Office of Education Performance Review.

Phi Delta Kappa. 1980. *Why Do Some Urban Schools Succeed? The Phi Delta Kappan Study of Exceptional Urban Elementary Schools.* Bloomington, Ind.: Phi Delta Kappa.

Rist, Ray. 1973. *The Urban School: A Factory of Failure.* Cambridge, Mass.: MIT.

Vallina, S. A. 1978. "Analysis of observed critical task performance of Title I-ESEA principals, State of Illinois." Ed.D. diss., Loyola University.

Venezsky, R. L., and L. Winfield. 1979. "Schools that succeed beyond expectations in teaching reading." Newark, Del.: University of Delaware Studies on Education, Technical Report no. 1.

Weber, G. 1971. *Inner City Children Can Be Taught to Read: Four Successful Schools.* Washington, D.C.: Council for Basic Education.

Wellisch, J. B., et al. 1978. "School management and organization in successful schools." *Sociology of Education* 51, no. 3: 211–26.

Wilson, K. 1982. "An effective school principal." *Educational Leadership* 39, no. 5: 357–61.

Wolfson, E. 1980. "An investigation of the relationship between elementary principal leadership styles and reading achievement of third and sixth grade students." Ph.D. diss., Hofstra University.

3

Framework for the Study

The works of C. I. Barnard (1947) and P. Selznick (1957) are consistent with the principal leadership literature; the desirable leadership qualities that these writers discuss are very similar to the qualities deemed important in the effective schools literature.

Barnard speaks of three major responsibilities leaders of organizations must possess—developing organizational goals, harnessing the energy of followers, and providing systems for internal communication (Barnard, 1947). A discussion of each responsibility follows.

In developing institutional goals, leaders need to keep two factors in mind. First, goals must be clearly developed and the leader must personally embody them. Second, in order for the goals to be realized, they must be accepted by all key actors. According to Selznick, a major mistake that leaders make is failing to set goals or having superficial ones (Selznick, 1957).

The essential strategy in harnessing the energy of followers is to achieve a consensus among the followers regarding the institutional goals and provide leadership in such a way that all of the actors do the work necessary to reach the stated goals.

Implicit in the need to harness the energy of the followers is the need to obtain internal sources of support by using existing groups and developing new ones. Leaders must make an impact upon the informal organization. They must be able to influence the various social groupings which develop within their staffs and contribute to the developments of such groups. For example, with homophily, workers may congregate according to age group. The leader must be able to interact effectively with each of these different groups in order to assure their adherence to institutional goals. This requires an understanding of the informal structure and consideration of the followers' personalities, problems, and interests. In effect, the leader must understand the role of human interactions—the fundamental basis for achieving institutional goals.

Formal organization, Barnard states, is calculated, considered, meaningful cooperation. Cooperation comes about when key actors in an organization strive to attain goals which require the input of other actors (Barnard, 1947). Harnessing the energy of followers is necessary to bring about this cooperation. Those who are neutral must be made committed and the energy of the isolated, the alienated, and the anomic must be corralled.

Providing a communication system is important because it enables the leader to articulate the institutional goals and to receive feedback from followers. Also, it enables the leader to get an indication of the mood of the followers with regard to their level of acceptance or rejection of the institutional goals at any given point (Barnard, 1947).

Selznick makes a key distinction between organizations and institutions. Organizations emphasize technical administrative management. Institutions, on the other hand, focus on maintaining institutional integrity. This integrity is the staff harmony that develops as a result of an organizational climate influencing and guiding attitudes, behaviors, and decisions, catapulting the organization to the level of institution (Selznick, 1957).

Barnard's role for leaders—defining goals, harnessing energies, and facilitating communication—can be regarded as the main ingredient in the maintenance of this institutional integrity. In schools, principals striving for this institutional integrity would need to clearly develop the school's goals, successfully encourage all staff to work harmoniously to reach the goals, and bring about two-way communication between themselves and the teachers.

VARIABLES TO BE CONSIDERED

My conceptual framework integrates the works of Barnard and Selznick with the literature on principal leadership and academic achievement. It concentrates on the following variables: (1) development of goals, (2) energy harnessing, (3) two-way communication facilitation, and (4) instructional management (see figure 3.1 for a depiction of the framework).

Goal Development

Leaders in more successful organizations construct goals that are easily understood and applied. Such leaders accept

Figure 3.1
Conceptual Framework

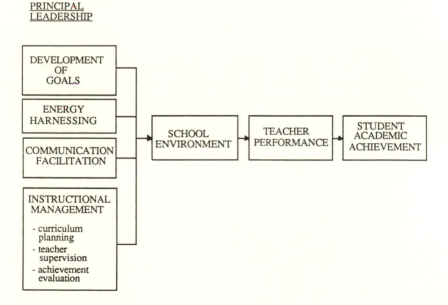

and personify these goals. Goal development is a variable included in the Barnard–Selznick framework. According to
Castetter (1976), an emphasis by principals on the development
of goals brings about the principal/teacher cooperation
necessary for teachers to be effective in facilitating high
academic achievement. With clear goals, principals are less inclined to have conflicts with teachers and teachers are more
likely to understand and internalize the goals. As a result,
teachers are better able to effectively interact with students,
contributing to the attainment of the desired goals. The
development of meaningful goals is important for any leader of
an effective organization (Selznick, 1957). Moreover, if a principal develops clear institutional goals, and personifies them
within the school, the likelihood is greater that teachers will
also embody these goals.

Energy Harnessing

In order to bring about the necessary cooperation that Barnard talks about, it is imperative that leaders capture the energy
of their followers and begin to challenge them into working
toward a collectively oriented direction. Castetter (1976) and
McGregor (1966) both support this contention in their works.
The ability to capture the energy of one's followers is fundamental in creating the staff harmony that is so important in
bringing about productivity (in this case, high academic
achievement). The ability of the principal to pull staff together
to strive for collective goals is key.

Communication Facilitation

Leaders must be able to effectively transfer to their workers
information regarding institutional goals. In addition, they
must make sure that there is ample opportunity and encourage-
ment for staff members to articulate their concerns regarding
the operation of the organization. Communication is important
to both Barnard and Selznick and also figures highly in other

research. Developing goals and harnessing energy are both important, but these accomplishments will be for naught in the absence of a functional two-way communication channel within the organization. Wellisch et al. (1978) found that the ability of a principal to communicate institutional goals effectively to staff, coupled with facilitation of staff feedback has an indirect, though clear and positive, effect on academic achievement. That is, if a principal regularly talks with teachers about issues such as teacher performance and curriculum development, there is a greater likelihood that the school will be more successful.

Instructional Management

This variable comes from the literature on principal leadership and academic achievement. Principals who exhibit this quality are intimately involved in the curriculum planning process through such activities as attending staff meetings and staying abreast of curriculum developments (California State Department of Education, 1980). These principals are also regularly involved in the supervision and evaluation of teacher performance (Wellisch et al. 1978). Such principals are regularly involved in the evaluation of academic achievement through such activities as monitoring schoolwide test results and reporting these results to teachers (Brookover and Lezotte, 1979).

California Assessment Program (CAP) Test

Studies examining the link between principal leadership and academic achievement invariably use standardized achievement test scores (Rowan, Bossert, and Dwyer, 1983). As a measure of school effectiveness, I utilized a composite of the third- and sixth-grade math and reading scale scores on the CAP test, for the school years 1980–81 and 1981–82.

The final formulation of my research questions is as follows:

1. How do African-American principals in more successful African-American elementary schools demonstrate goal development, energy harnessing, communication facilitation, and instructional management (i.e., regular involvement in (a) the evaluation of academic achievement, (b) curriculum planning, and (c) teacher supervision) in their schools?

2. How does the leadership of African-American principals in more successful African-American elementary schools compare with the leadership of other principals as described in the research literature on principal leadership and academic achievement?

3. What other leadership qualities, if any, do African-American principals in more successful African-American elementary schools hold in common with each other?

REFERENCES

Barnard, C. I. 1947. *The Functions of the Executive.* Cambridge, Mass.: Harvard University Press.

Brookover, W., and L. W. Lezotte. 1979. "Changes in school characteristics coincident with changes in student achievement." East Lansing: Michigan State University, College of Urban Development.

California State Department of Education. 1980. *1977 California School Effectiveness Study. The First Year: 1974–75.* Sacramento, Calif.: Office of Program Evaluation and Research.

Castetter, W. B. 1976. *The Personnel Function in Educational Administration.* New York: Macmillan.

McGregor, D. 1966. *Leadership and Motivation.* Cambridge, Mass.: MIT.

Rowan, B., S. T. Bossert, D. C. Dwyer. 1983. "Research on effective schools: A cautionary note." *Educational Researcher* 12, no. 4: 24–31.

Selznick, P. 1957. *Leadership in Administration: A Sociological Interpretation.* Evanston, Ill.: Row, Peterson.

Wellisch, J. B., et al. 1978. "School management and organization in successful schools." *Sociology of Education* 51, no. 3: 211–26.

4

Methods of the Study

OVERVIEW

This book reports on a study of the relationship between the leadership of African-American principals and African-American student academic achievement in more successful African-American elementary schools in the state of California. I attempted to determine how the principals in my sample exhibited four components of leadership style: (1) development of goals, (2) energy harnessing, (3) communication facilitation, and (4) instructional management. In addition, I sought to identify other facets of leadership that may affect students' academic achievement.

My strategy began with the identification of the population of African-American elementary schools in the state of California. Next, I selected a sample of four more successful schools whose principals had been in their present positions at least since the 1978–79 academic year. I sought this tenure in order to be able to explore the link between the success of the school and the current principal's leadership.

I interviewed teachers and principals, observed the principals at work, and used teacher questionnaires to examine how the principals implemented the four components of leadership. The data analysis was qualitative.

SAMPLING PROCEDURE

I started with a list of 142 African-American elementary schools in the state of California. This list was provided by the Office of Intergroup Relations in the California Department of Education. From phone calls, I found out that 93 of these 142 schools had African-American principals, and that in 26 of these 93 schools, the principals had been in their present position since the 1978–79 school year.

In order to rank the schools, an unweighted sum was computed (for each of the remaining 26 schools) of the third- and sixth-grade combined reading and math scale scores on CAP tests for 1980–81 and 1981–82. The math and reading scores were added together to form a composite. The use of an unweighted sum as a composite of the math and reading scale scores was appropriate, as the scores for each subject area were scaled with the same variance. As a result, the math and reading scores were comparable. By using math and reading, third and sixth grades, and two consecutive years, I obtained a more dependable, broader base of comparison. The use of two subject areas limits the possibility of obtaining results that might be idiosyncratic for one particular subject area. Using two grade levels also adds dependability to the measure as any peculiar explanations for scores on one grade level may not apply to another level. Finally, the use of scores from two years was a precaution, considering the possibility of one year's scores being unique. This is particularly relevant in many African-American schools, such as the ones used in this study, where there is a high level of student turnover.

Schools were then ranked based upon these composite scores. The nine schools in the top one-third of this distribution were classified as more successful, and the first four were selected for the study. An effort was made to insure that the selected schools were not unusually large or small or in atypical locations. Research has shown that factors such as school size and student socioeconomic status may have an impact upon principal leadership (Martinko and Gardner, 1983). The result

Table 4.1

Comparison of Test Scores of Sample Schools and California State Averages (1980–81/1981–82)

1980-81

	Reading		Math	
	3rd	6th	3rd	6th
Collins Elementary School	194	209	206	237
Woodson Elementary School	233	211	218	218
Foster Elementary School	208	205	226	222
State Averages	254	252	254	253

1981-82

	Reading		Math	
	3rd	6th	3rd	6th
Collins Elementary School	187	205	215	218
Woodson Elementary School	199	212	202	213
Foster Elementary School	208	207	206	216
State Averages	258	254	261	258

was a sample containing four more successful African-American elementary schools with African-American principals who had held their current positions from at least the 1978–79 academic year through the 1984–85 academic year. It should be noted that when comparing these more successful African-American schools with the overall state distribution of elementary schools, they fall significantly below the average (see table 4.1 for a summary of the comparison). Still, something important can be learned from these schools, as they represent the best of the African-American schools.

During my initial observations, the principal from what was to have been my fourth school cancelled his participation in the study. I had previously identified other principals in case somebody dropped out, but at this point, all of the remaining principals whose schools were eligible for my study (those in the top one-third of the distribution) were no longer at their schools. Therefore I decided to limit the sample to three principals. No serious problems were caused by this alteration as I still had enough variability to have descriptive power in the study. That is, with three principals, I was able to compare and contrast differing styles in a manner sufficient to allow for a meaningful analysis.

MEASUREMENT PROCEDURE

Instrumentation

I conducted a pilot study in an African-American elementary school in a northern California school district. The purpose of this pilot study was twofold: (1) to determine the usefulness of the individual questions in the questionnaire and the interviews which were to be used in data collection; and (2) to aid me in becoming more comfortable and better prepared to conduct the observations in the full-scale study.

I used four primary data-gathering techniques to examine each of the four principal qualities. The entire faculty of each school was asked to complete a teacher questionnaire that had been adapted from P. Hallinger (see appendix A for a list of the questions on the questionnaire). In Hallinger's dissertation, he identifies eleven areas of principal leadership (Hallinger, 1983). I used thirty-two of his seventy-nine questions and formulated eighteen additional questions for use in my four categories. There was a composite 73 percent return rate on the questionnaire (twenty of twenty-three or 87 percent at Collins; sixteen of twenty-seven or 59 percent at Woodson; and eleven of fourteen or 79 percent at Foster).

A sample of teachers was chosen as respondents and I conducted teacher interviews of approximately thirty minutes in length. The sessions were in closed classrooms and were tape-recorded (see appendix B for a list of the questions asked during the teacher interviews). In meetings with the staffs of each of the schools, I asked for volunteers to be interviewed and chose additional respondents until I had five at each school. One concern was whether the nonrandom sample would bias the results. The results of the interviews were consistent with the results of the other instruments, supporting my contention that the sample was representative (see appendix C for a comparison of the results of each of the instruments).

I conducted two-day direct, structured observations of each of the principals in the fall of 1984 and again in the winter of 1985. Each principal was observed for a total of four full days. Observations of a four-day duration are unusually short. However, some researchers have conducted studies with similar lengths of observations (Lightfoot, 1983; Mintzberg, 1973; Pitner, 1978). In addition, the circumstances in this case warranted this exception. I began my data collection with a clear description of the variables that I intended to examine. This clarity derived from a detailed reading of the relevant research literature and the related theoretical constructs leading to the development of my framework. In addition, the fact that I had three additional instruments and that I repeated the observations helped to justify brief observations.

The repetition of the observations was a precaution. Previous researchers have concluded that the time of year may significantly affect leadership activity in jobs that have regularly recurring cycles, such as the academic year (Larsen et al., 1981). Generally, I wanted to compensate for the possibility that what I observed during my first set of observations was atypical. Also, observers effects tend to be minimized with repeated observations (Borg and Gall, 1979; Wolcott, 1973). I unobtrusively followed and observed the principals and I kept descriptive notes. I followed each principal for a full work day or, on an average, nine hours.

I also conducted principal interviews with each principal (see appendix D for a list of the questions asked during the principal interviews). In addition to the interviews, observations, and questionnaires, I spent about twenty hours in or around each school observing recesses, classes, and lunch periods, and talking informally with students, teachers, and staff about their work and the school. The intent was to obtain an overall picture of the schools and to collect any additional, useful data that may not have been obtained with the four primary instruments. Also, an attempt was made to collect relevant documents. I was able to obtain some documents, particularly lists of school goals for each school.

Goal Development

Data collection in this area focused on the existence of goals, ascertaining how they were formulated and how easy they were to understand.

In the teacher questionnaire, there were seven questions which focused on this quality. The first two were general, while the remaining questions focused on the teacher's perceptions of their principal.

Teacher Questionnaire

a. Does your school have goals?   yes   no

b. How familiar are you with your school's goals?   1 2 3 4 5 6

c. Frames the school's goals with target dates   1 2 3 4 5 6

d. Frames the school's goals in terms of staff responsibilities for meeting them   1 2 3 4 5 6

e. Develops goals that are easily translated into
   classroom objectives by teachers   1 2 3 4 5 6

f. Develops goals that seek improvement over current levels of performance   1 2 3 4 5 6

g. Uses data on student performance when developing school goals   1 2 3 4 5 6

Teacher Interview

a. Do you have goals at your school?

b. In what areas have goals been formulated?

c. What are these goals?

d. Are these goals written?

e. Do you have a copy of them?

f. How were these goals formulated?

g. Who was involved in their formulation?

h. How effective have these goal-formulation procedures been?

i. What have been some of your school's least effective ways of dealing with goal formulation?

j. In your view, how important are these goals in the daily operation of your school?

Principal Interview

a. Do you have goals at your school?

b. In what areas have goals been formulated?

c. What are these goals?

d. Are these goals written?

e. May I have a copy of them?

f. How were they formulated?

g. Who was involved in their formulation?

h. How effective have your procedures for goal formulation been?

i. What have been some of your least effective ways of dealing with goal formulation?

j. How important are these goal in the daily operation of your school?

Energy Harnessing

Energy harnessing involves the degree to which principals draw staff together to work cooperatively toward the realization of the school's goals. I explored the tactics employed by the principals to attempt to bring about this cooperation.

In the teacher questionnaire, there were ten questions that focused on this quality. The first two were general while questions c through j focused on the teachers' perception of their principal's leadership in this area.

Teacher Questionnaire

a. Does your principal attempt to affect the behavior of staff members who may not be in line with the school's goals?   yes   no

b. How effective would you say your principal has been in such situations?   1 2 3 4 5 6

c. Keeps staff working together as a team   1 2 3 4 5 6

d. Has support of key teachers/teacher groups   1 2 3 4 5 6

e. Distributes notes, announcements, or newsletters to teachers informing them of opportunities for professional development that are related to the school's goals   1 2 3 4 5 6

f. Selects in-service activities that are consistent with the school's goals   1 2 3 4 5 6

g. Distributes journal articles to teachers on a regular basis   1 2 3 4 5 6

h. Ensures that instructional aides receive appropriate training to help students meet instructional objectives   1 2 3 4 5 6

i. Arranges for outside speakers to make presentations on instructional issues at faculty meetings   1 2 3 4 5 6

j. Provides time to meet individually with teachers to discuss instructional issues   1 2 3 4 5 6

Teacher Interview

a. To your knowledge, does your principal attempt to affect the behavior of staff members who are not necessarily in line with the school's goals?

b. In what ways does your principal approach such a situation?

c. What have been some of your principal's most effective strategies?

d. What have been some of your principal's least effective strategies?

Principal Interview

a. Do you attempt to affect the behavior of staff members who are not in line with the school's goals?
b. In what ways do you approach such a situation?
c. What have been some of your most effective strategies?
d. What have been some of your least effective strategies?

Communication Facilitation

I focused here on the existence of such communication (i.e., does the principal articulate the goals?) and on the strategies used by the principals to stimulate two-way communication with staff in such areas as goals and school policies.

In the teacher questionnaire, four questions were general, while the remainder focused on teachers' perceptions of their principal.

Teacher Questionnaire

a. Does your principal attempt to communicate the school's goals to staff? yes   no

b. How effective would you say your principal has been in this communication? 1 2 3 4 5 6

c. Do teachers in your school attempt to offer feedback on goals, school policies, etc.? yes   no

d. How effective are teachers in these attempts? 1 2 3 4 5 6

e. Refers to school goals in informal settings with teachers 1 2 3 4 5 6

f. Refers to school goals at faculty meetings 1 2 3 4 5 6

g. Refers to school goals when making curricular decisions with teachers 1 2 3 4 5 6

h. Ensures that the school goals are reflected in highly visible displays in the school (e.g., posters and bulletin boards) indicating the importance of reading and/or math   1 2 3 4 5 6

i. Refers to school goals in assemblies   1 2 3 4 5 6

j. Keeps staff well informed   1 2 3 4 5 6

k. Is easy to understand   1 2 3 4 5 6

l. Is generally knowledgeable of staff personalities, problems, and interests   1 2 3 4 5 6

m. Uses needs assessment or other questionnaire to secure staff input on goal development   1 2 3 4 5 6

n. Finds time to listen to staff members   1 2 3 4 5 6

o. Looks out for personal welfare of individual staff members   1 2 3 4 5 6

p. Is friendly and approachable   1 2 3 4 5 6

q. Makes staff members feel at ease when talking to them   1 2 3 4 5 6

Teacher Interview

a. Are you aware of any attempts by your principal to communicate the school's goals to staff? If yes, please describe these attempts.

b. What have been some of your principal's most useful methods of communication?

c. What have been some of your principal's least useful methods of communication?

d. Do teachers offer feedback on school policies, goals, etc.?

e. What channels are used for this feedback?

f. Are the teachers' channels effective?

g. Are the teachers' channels sufficient?

Principal Interview

a. Do you attempt to communicate the school's goals to staff?

b. How do you attempt this?

c. What have been some of your most useful
   methods of communicating?

d. What have been some of your least useful methods
   of communicating?

e. Do teachers offer feedback on school policies,
   goals, etc.?

f. What channels are used for this feedback?

g. Are the teachers' channels sufficient?

In assessing the instructional management of the principals, I used each instrument to note the methods employed by the principals in the areas of curriculum planning, teacher supervision, and the evaluation of student achievement. I focused on the degree to which the principals were engaged in these activities. There were two general questions on the teacher questionnaire.

a. Do you view your principal as an instructional
   manager?   yes   no

b. How would you rate your principal's instructional
   management skills?   1 2 3 4 5 6

Instructional Management: Curriculum Planning

Here I focused on how deeply the principal was involved in curriculum planning, whether the principal attended curriculum planning meetings, and whether he or she tended to stay abreast of new curriculum developments.

In the teacher questionnaire, all of the questions focused on teacher perceptions of their principal's leadership.

Teacher Questionnaire

a. Makes clear to teachers who is reponsible for
   coordinating curriculum content across grade
   levels (e.g., the principal, the vice principal, or a
   teacher)   1 2 3 4 5 6

b. Participates in meetings for the purpose of reviewing or selecting instructional materials   1 2 3 4 5 6

c. Ensures that the goals of the school are translated into common curricular objectives   1 2 3 4 5 6

d. Draws upon the results of schoolwide testing when making curricular decisions   1 2 3 4 5 6

e. Ensures that the content selected from textbooks by teachers is aligned with the school's goals   1 2 3 4 5 6

Teacher Interview

a. What are the procedures for curriculum planning at your school?
b. Who is involved in these procedures?
c. How effective are these methods?

Principal Interviews

a. What are the procedures for curriculum planning at your school?
b. Who is involved in these procedures?
c. How effective are these procedures?

Instructional Management: Teacher Supervision

There were no questions on the teacher questionnaire that focused on teacher supervision. Data for this variable was gathered primarily through principal observations.

There were no questions in the teacher interview that focused on teacher supervision. However, some information was gained during the interviews that was useful in exploring this area.

There were no questions in the principal interview that focused on teacher supervision. However, again, some useful data on this variable were gained during the principal interviews.

Instructional Management: Evaluation of Student Achievement

The concern here was whether the principal monitored schoolwide tests and whatever follow-up occurred after the results were received by the school.

In the teacher questionnaire, all of the questions focused on teachers' perceptions of their principal's leadership.

Teacher Questionnaire

a. Assesses agreement between school's goals and the achievement test(s) used for program evaluation
1 2 3 4 5 6

b. Meets individually with teachers to discuss pupil academic performance
1 2 3 4 5 6

c. Discusses the item analysis of schoolwide tests such as the CAP with the faculty in order to identify strengths and weaknesses in the school's program
1 2 3 4 5 6

d. Uses the results of schoolwide testing to assess progress toward school goals
1 2 3 4 5 6

e. Distributes the results of student testing to teachers in a timely fashion
1 2 3 4 5 6

f. Informs teachers of the school's performance results on tests in written form (e.g., memos or newsletters)
1 2 3 4 5 6

g. Informs students of the school's performance results
1 2 3 4 5 6

h. Identifies students whose performance on school tests indicates the need for special instruction such as remediation or enrichment
1 2 3 4 5 6

i. Develops or finds appropriate instructional programs for students whose performance on tests indicates a need
1 2 3 4 5 6

Teacher Interview

a. In your school, how is the evaluation of achievement handled?

b. Who is involved in this process?

c. How effective is this process?

Principal Interview

a. In your school, how is the evaluation of achievement handled?

b. Who is involved in this process?

c. How effective is this process?

Academic Achievement

Success in student academic achievement was assessed by noting the level at which students performed on a standardized achievement test in the areas of math and reading over a two-year period. I used a composite score for each school based on combined math and reading scale scores of the CAP test for grades three and six for the school years 1980–81 and 1981–82.

The CAP test is administered annually to all third- and sixth-grade students in all California public elementary schools. It measures basic skills in reading, written language, and mathematics. I did not use the written language battery. I excluded these scores from the composite because there is little research utilizing this indicator as a measure of academic achievement.

Observations. Time limitations suggested the utilization of structured observations. The four variables described earlier were employed to guide data collection. This enabled me to collect data selectively, minimizing data overload and to do comparisons across sites. The sampling frame for the observations included settings, actors, events, and processes. The settings were everywhere principals went during the course of the day except when they did something that was in no way related to their job (e.g., family errands and personal business meetings) or on the few occasions when I was asked to absent myself for whatever reason. The actors included the principals and everyone with whom they came in contact during the day in the course of their work. Events were those in which the principals participated as school leaders. Processes were all the things the principals did in their capacity as school leader.

During the observations, I took extensive notes on what the principals did and noted my own interpretations and perceptions. I developed a coding system so that following each day's observations I could, after editing the raw data, code the information into categories related to my four areas of interest. I recorded all of the behavior which I observed during my observations, focusing on behavior that appeared to be related to the four qualities under examination. After looking at my first few sets of observation notes, I established the following categories of activities:

1. Talking with someone outside of the school community
2. Dealing with curriculum (e.g., book selection, course evaluation)
3. Classroom observations
4. Dealing with discipline
5. Doing desk work (e.g., opening mail, signing letters)
6. In the school yard
7. Having social discussions with staff person(s)
8. Talking with researcher
9. Instructional time (teaching a class)
10. Talking with a teacher or administrator

Next I designated the leadership categories as follows:

A. Goal development
B. Energy harnessing
C. Communication facilitation
D. Curriculum planning
E. Teacher supervision
F. Evaluation of student achievement

Finally, I went through my notes and coded each entry. If a principal was talking with a teacher about school goals, I would code the activity 10C. Similarly, in instances where the principal was discussing a child with a teacher and was focusing on the goals of the school with regard to, say, emphasizing self-worth, I coded them 10C.

If the principal was talking with a teacher about some classroom responsibility such as following up on a reading diagnosis, I coded it 10E. Similarly, whenever the principal asked a teacher to do a task related to his or her job, I coded it 10E.

All classroom observations, no matter how long or how structured, which the principal conducted, were coded 3E. Discussions that the principal had with teachers or members of the administrative staff related to the use of texts or other areas of curricular decision making were coded 10D.

Sometimes social discussions seemed to serve the purpose of communication facilitation, either because the principal used the opportunity to stress some specific goal(s) or because it appeared to facilitate a sense of comfort on the part of the teacher in offering feedback. These instances were coded 7C.

Often gatherings, formal or informal, of more than one teacher and the principal were geared toward getting the staff to agree to work together on a particular task or to begin to behave in a particular way. In these cases, it often appeared as though the principal was attempting to harness the energy of the teachers around the goals of the school. In instances where this appeared to be the case, they were coded 10B.

Behaviors or activities that did not appear to be directly related to the qualities under examination were not coded as conscientiously as those that did appear as such. For example, I paid less attention to instances where the principals were talking to their office managers than I did to instances where they were talking to teachers. If, in fact, an encounter with an office manager appeared related to one of the qualities under examination, I did note it.

Teacher Questionnaires. Responses on the questionnaire ranged from 1 to 5 or from "almost never" to "almost always."[1] Once I determined the mean value for each principal for each response, I set the cut-off point at 3.9. The 3.9 cutoff was selected because, based upon the coding scheme used on the questionnaire, a 4 was considered to mean "frequently." I felt therefore that if a principal scored less than "frequently" on a given area that I would consider that particular trait absent. For example, Mr. Charles received a mean score of 3.4 on the question "keeps staff well informed." I therefore assumed that this instrument suggested that he did not have this quality. The same criteria was set up for groups of questions related to a particular quality (e.g., goal development). For example, Ms. Marshall's mean score for all of the questions in the goal development category was 4.4. Consequently, I had support for the assertion that she provided leadership in this area.

Principal and Teacher Interviews. A similar, though somewhat more subjective, coding criteria was used for the interviews. I ranked the verbal responses of the respondents. For example, in listening to a teacher's response to the question, "Does your principal attempt to affect the behavior of teachers who may not be in line with the school's goals?," I rated the response from 1 to 5, again with 1 being "almost never" and 5 being "almost always." Again, a mean score for each principal in each category of questions was determined and I used these additional data to support my concluding observations.

The information obtained from the principal interviews and the teacher interviews was used, along with the information from the teacher questionnaire, to supplement the observation data.

RELIABILITY AND VALIDITY

M. B. Miles and A. M. Huberman (1984) suggest that four qualities in a qualitative researcher can aid in increasing reliability and validity: (1) familiarity with the phenomenon under study, (2) strong conceptual interests, (3) a multidisciplinary approach, and (4) good investigative skills.

Reliability

There are two kinds of reliability. External reliability is the degree to which a study can be replicated. That is, this kind of reliability addresses the issue of whether another researcher using the same methods could obtain the same results (LeCompte and Goetz, 1982). Qualitative research, however, is conducted in a natural, unique setting which is, by definition, unreconstructable, ruling out the possibility of identical results (Jick, 1979). In fact, in the behavioral sciences, replication is generally rare and difficult to obtain (Cronbach, 1951).

Internal reliability, or interrater reliability, is the degree to which another researcher, given constructs, would match them with data in a way similar to that of the original researcher (LeCompte and Goetz, 1982). This is an appropriate concept for a study such as this one. However, at this point it would be difficult to consider the extent to which another observer would agree with my perceptions of the settings and with my conclusions, since there were no other observers involved in the study.

The ability of subsequent observers to replicate the findings of studies such as this one is dependent upon the degree to which the analytical strategies are specified in the original research. I have included an abundance of primary data, particularly from principal and teacher interviews. Such data, referred to as low-inference descriptors, tend to reduce threats to internal reliability (LeCompte and Goetz, 1982).

Validity

There are two kinds of validity. Internal validity is the degree to which the data are unbiased and undistorted. That is, it is the degree to which the data are authentic representations of a given reality (Dawson, 1978; LeCompte and Goetz, 1982; Cronbach, 1951). External validity is the degree to which the results can be generalized to other populations (Dawson, 1978; LeCompte and Goetz, 1982). The use of four data collection methods serves to increase internal validity. This technique, known as between-method triangulation, presumably allows researchers to compensate for the weaknesses of a given method with the strengths of the other methods. As a result, it is more difficult to attribute the findings to the idiosyncrasies of a given method (Jick, 1979).

In addition, in this study, I made efforts to establish conditions conducive to the collection of valid data. For example, I attempted to establish trusting relationships with the respondents.[2] Presumably, such relationships bring about more honest, complete responses than might otherwise be the case (Dawson, 1978). The efforts that I made to establish trusting relationships with the respondents were consistent with the suggestions of J. Dean, R. Eichhorn, and L. Dean (1967). I began by contacting the district offices and then the principals (starting from the top down). I focused on the need to gain more information about the education of African-American children (a concern that I perceived to be sensible and plausible in the eyes of the respondents). I presented an honest representation of myself. I began with routine fact-finding questions in the interviews (see appendices B and D). Finally, I felt as though my presence was legitimatized, in the eyes of the respondents, by my affiliation with Stanford University and by a genuine interest, on my part, in their work in their schools.

Other considerations in qualitative research that tend to increase internal validity include: (1) longer periods of data collection, aiding in the refining of constructs to enable them to align more closely with reality; (2) less abstract instrumentation (e.g., interviews are phrased close to the categories); (3) observations in a natural, uncontrived setting; and (4) a constant reevaluation of the data generated by the research.

The issue of external validity or the ability to generalize is of unique significance in qualitative studies. In such studies, the attempt is to be able to generalize to theoretical and empirical literature rather than to populations. The inquiry aims at obtaining results that can be compared to, in my case, effective schools research as it relates to principal leadership. As a result, my conclusions are phrased in terms related to such comparisons and are not geared toward generalizing to populations.

Limitations

While reliability and validity are issues that can be accounted for and justified, there are some limitations to the study.

There have been problems cited in the past regarding the use of standardized test scores as a measure of effectiveness. One concern is that these scores provide a limited definition of effectiveness, often in conflict with the perceptions of practitioners who focus on organizational, social, and emotional domains when considering effectiveness (Lightfoot, 1983, Purkey and Smith, 1982). Limitations prevented me from developing a more comphrehensive (and perhaps more meaningful) measure. However, I wanted to explore the influence of African-American principals in effective African-American schools using measurements common in school effectiveness research.

One may not, of course, generalize with any confidence from an N-3 study to a wide population. The aim in this study, however, is for comparability and translatability, not generalizability (LeCompte and Goetz, 1982). The intent was to describe the characteristics of the principals and schools clearly so that the descriptions could serve as a basis for comparison with other principals and schools. Also, I wanted to provide explicit descriptions enabling confidence in future comparisons. I do offer some propositions based upon my analysis of Foster, Woodson, and Collins Elementary Schools which may guide other schools as they seek to become more successful. Also, I hope my analysis highlights themes worthy of further study. If my descriptions of these three principals and their schools help anyone else in another elementary school, that is a more appropriate form of utility.

The intent of this study was to compare the leadership of African-American principals in more successful African-American elementary schools with the leadership of other principals in elementary schools described as effective in the literature. I wanted to see if this body of literature on principal leadership and academic achievement held any relevance for African-American principals in African-American schools. Still, the study would have been stronger had there been a comparison of African-American and white principals. Such a comparison would have given greater credibility to speculations growing out of the study regarding the leadership of African-American principals. That is, any qualities that the African-American principals appeared to possess could more easily be attributed to their race if a comparison group of white principals failed to show the same qualities.

Similarly, a comparison of African-American principals in more successful African-American elementary schools and those in less successful African-American elementary schools would have given additional support for conclusions regarding the leadership of African-American principals in more successful African-American elementary schools. If the qualities that I attributed to African-American principals in more successful African-American elementary schools were not held by the principals in the less successful African-American elementary schools, speculation regarding the leadership of African-American principals in more successful African-American elementary schools could be made stronger.

NOTES

1. Actually, there was a 6 on the questionnaire, but the 6 was reserved for instances where the respondent, for whatever reason, felt that he or she could not appropriately answer the question. For the purposes of obtaining a mean score for coding, these responses were considered "no responses," and were not included in the analysis.

2. Though my actual observations of each principal lasted for only four days (two days in the fall and two days in the winter of the 1984–85 academic year), I made initial contact with each principal in the spring of the 1983–84 academic year and talked with each of them regularly (at least once a month) through the 1984–85 academic year. In addition, I was at each school for a full week in the fall and winter and on the days when I was not observing the principals, I spent additional time with them, talking about the school and about other less formal issues.

REFERENCES

Borg, W. R., and M. D. Gall. 1979. *Educational Research: An Introduction.* New York: Longman.

Cronbach, L. J. 1951. "Coefficient alpha and the internal structure of tests." *Psychometrika* 16, no. 3: 297–334.

Dawson, J. A. 1978. "Validity in qualitative research." Mimeographed chapter of manuscript.

Dean, J., R. Eichorn, and L. Dean, 1967. "Fruitful informants for intensive interviewing." In J. T. Doby, ed., *An Introduction to Social Research*. New York: Meredith.

Hallinger, P. 1983. "Assessing the instructional management behavior of principals." Ed. D. diss., Stanford University.

Jick, T. D. 1979. "Mixing qualitative and quantitative methods: Triangulation in action. "*Administrative Science Quarterly* 24, no. 4: 602–11.

Larsen, L. L., et al. 1981. *The Nature of a School Superintendent's Work: Final Technical Report*. Carbondale: Southern Illinois University.

LeCompte, M. D., and J. P. Goetz. 1982. "Problems of reliability and validity in ethnographic research." *Review of Educational Research* 52, no. 1:31–60.

Lightfoot, S. L. 1983. *The Good High School*. New York: Basic.

Martinko, W., and W. Gardner. 1983. "The behavior of high performing educational managers: An observational study." Working Paper. Tallahassee, Florida State University.

Miles, M. B., and A. M. Huberman. 1984. *Qualitative Data Analysis: A Sourcebook of New Methods*. Beverly Hills: Sage.

Mintzberg, H. 1973. *The Nature of Managerial Work*. New York: Harper and Row.

Pitner, N. J. 1978. "Descriptive study of the everyday activities of suburban school superintendents: The management of information." Ph.D. diss., Ohio State University.

Purkey, S. C., and M. S. Smith. 1982. "Effective schools—A review." Paper presented at NIE Conference on "Research in Teaching: Implications for Practice." Warrenton, Va.

Wolcott, H. F. 1973. *The Man in the Principal's Office: An Ethnography*. New York: Holt, Rinehart and Winston.

5

Profiles of Schools

MARCUS COLLINS ELEMENTARY SCHOOL

Setting

Marcus Collins Elementary School is located in an urban area with a population of over 2.5 million. It is in the Accra Unified School District in southern California.[1] It is in a community made up primarily of small, single-family homes.

Collins Elementary School consists of two main buildings connected by a patiolike walkway. There are three bungalows behind the main buidings with two classrooms in each. The buildings and grounds are clean. The buildings were recently painted. It was very quiet inside and there were few wall hangings.

There were no parking areas for staff on the grounds. However, plans were being made to remove four of the portable classrooms and to build a staff parking lot. The schoolyard had concrete ground with areas marked off for basketball, softball, and other activities.

Teachers

The typical teacher at Collins had worked there for three years, but averaged fourteen years of total teaching experience.

Table 5.1

Comparison of Racial Composition of Sample Schools and Their Home Districts—Students and Teachers (in percentages)

	Native American	White	Asian	Black	Hispanic	Total
Accra Unified School District						
Students	0.7	33.6	6.1	24.5	34.8	100.0
Teachers	0.9	69.7	6.3	16.7	6.1	100.0
Marcus Collins Elementary School						
Students	0.0	0.0	0.0	85.0	15.0	100.0
Teachers	0.0	70.8	4.2	25.0	0.0	100.0
Bole Unified School District						
Students	0.2	6.2	1.5	80.8	11.2	100.0
Teachers	0.3	60.8	4.0	31.9	2.8	100.0
Marva Woodson Elementary School						
Students	0.0	2.0	1.0	65.0	32.0	100.0
Teachers	0.0	33.3	4.2	54.2	8.3	100.0
Kumasi Unified School District						
Students	0.3	61.6	2.2	10.3	25.4	100.0
Teachers	0.4	86.6	2.0	4.9	5.8	100.0
Carter G. Foster Elementary School						
Students	0.0	0.0	8.0	66.0	26.0	100.0
Teachers	0.0	71.4	0.8	28.6	0.0	100.0

Almost one-half of the twenty-three teachers were in their first year. Sixteen teachers were white, six were African-American and one was Asian (see table 5.1 for a comparison of each school's teacher and student racial composition with their home district).

In the staff lounge during lunch, white and African-American teachers sit separately. Also administrators sit apart, as do office staff and kitchen staff. Rarely did these groups mingle during my visits.

Students

Eighty-five percent of the students at Collins were African-American with the remaining 15 percent being Hispanic. Over the last several years enrollment had remained relatively constant at about five hundred. During 1984–85 there were 581 students. The district average for elementary schools was 720. As a proxy for socioeconomic status, I determined that 481 students (83 percent) received free lunches at Collins.

Parents

Approximately thirty parents attended PTA meetings. A similar number volunteered at the school in various capacities. Parents made up two-thirds of the staff of aides at Collins. Most parents at Collins were employed and slightly under 40 percent of the students lived in single-parent homes.

During my observations the large majority of the contacts the principal seemed to have with parents was when there was a student discipline problem. On several occasions, however, I observed teachers talking with parents. One teacher showed me a letter from a parent praising the teacher for her fine work with her son.

Principal

The principal, Arthur Charles, was married and lived seventy-five miles from the school. He flew his own plane to school every day. He lived on a ranch with deer, pheasant, raccoons, dogs, and other wildlife. A man in his early sixties, he had sixteen years of teaching and fifteen years of administrative experience. He had been at Collins since 1976. He holds an LL.B. and has taken over twenty-five hours of administrative courses.

Mr. Charles' office had four plants, two of which were on his desk. On the wall were two pictures of planes and one of a bird. On the days that I observed there were no papers on his desk, only two books (*The Case For Character Education* and *The Teaching of Values*), a desk calendar, and the plants. One of the plants hid two vertical files, each containing a few papers.

Many staff members at Collins were quick to point out that, in their school, the principal was an excellent delegator and that much of the administrative work at Collins was handled by the coordinator and the resource teachers.

During my visits, the majority of Mr. Charles' time was spent talking with me in his office, sitting in the teachers' lounge, observing classes, and talking with parents and/or students regarding discipline.

Generally, Mr. Charles arrived at school at 8 A.M.. By 4 P.M., he was ready to depart. A typical day was as follows:

8:00 discipline problem with student and parent

8:20 spontaneous socializing in office with PTA president

8:30 general discussion with researcher

9:00 opening mail

9:15 teacher in office with request

9:25 observing classes

10:10 teacher in for request

10:20 to teachers' lounge for break with Title I coordinator and researcher with snack and general discussion

11:15 discipline problem with student

11:35 general discussion with researcher

12:30 to teachers' lounge for lunch with Title I coordinator and researcher—general discussion

1:30 answers one phone call and places another

1:45 general discussion with researcher

2:25 discussion with teacher regarding earlier classroom observation

2:45 Title I coordinator in to remind principal of special schedule for the next day

2:55 general discussion with researcher

3:30 Title I coordinator in to discuss plan for newly hired teacher

4:00 departure

Several teachers informed me that Mr. Charles rarely visited classrooms and that, in general, his behavior during my fall visit (i.e., regularly visiting classrooms) was atypical. His daily routine changed for my winter visit. He spent significantly less time observing classes.

MARVA WOODSON ELEMENTARY SCHOOL

Setting

Marva Woodson Elementary School is located in a highly transient community dominated by apartment houses in a large southern California city of ninety thousand. Most businesses in the community are small, typified by a Seven-Eleven store. The school is in the Bole Unified School District.

Woodson is in one building with twenty-one classrooms. It was overcrowded, yet neat and clean. A beautiful mural was on one of the outside walls of the school. It had not been defaced, according to the principal. There were six portable classrooms, but there were still not enough rooms for the school's current enrollment. In October 1984, two classes met in one room, and another class met in the school library. In January 1985, the situation had not changed considerably.

Teachers

The average teacher at Woodson had worked there for four years and had a total of fifteen years of teaching experience. Fifteen teachers were African-American, ten were white, one was Asian, and one was Hispanic. There was little racial segregation in the staff lounge. Teachers sat, seemingly, in the first available seat. In addition, the principal was almost always at a table with teachers. On several occasions, I observed teachers starting conversations with the principal. They would often sit down with her.

Students

The student population at Woodson was 65 percent African-American, 32 percent Hispanic, 2 percent white, and 1 percent Asian. Woodson had an enrollment of 798 students. The district average was 645. The students felt free to come to the principal's office to discuss anything with her or just to say hello.

A high level of instability in the larger community had, in the previous four years, led to a student turnover problem at Woodson. In 1983–84, only eighteen children from the previous year's three fifth-grade classes returned to Woodson. During 1982–83, student turnover peaked at 70 percent. While school socioeconomic status was unavailable, I did find out that 80 percent of the students at Woodson received free lunches during the 1984–85 school year.

Parents

Most of the parents of students at Woodson were employed. Where there were two parents in the home (a situation experienced by less than twenty of the almost eight-hundred students at Woodson) both usually worked.

There were no regularly scheduled PTA meetings. Parents had decided several years ago that the streets were too dangerous at night to travel back and forth to meetings. However, at special programs such as open school night, there were usually about 450 parents in attendance, according to the principal.

Until recently, all of the aides at Woodson were parents of students at the school. When I visited, slightly less than one-half of the aides were parents. Approximately ten parents helped out in classes and in other capacities around the school. Most of them were parents of new students in kindergarten. Parents did come in to talk with teachers and the principal.

Principal

The principal, Ms. Chesley Marshall, age forty-four, was married. She drove forty-five miles to work each day. She is a personable, energetic woman who stated during our interview that "instead of being a curriculum leader, you've got to be a curriculum leader and doer." She had served in her present capacity since 1976. Ms. Marshall holds an M.S.Ed., and had thirteen years of teaching experience and nine years of administrative experience.

Ms. Marshall is a particularly well-dressed woman with smartly matched attire and accessories. Her early mornings were typified by her putting on her make-up in front of the mirror in her office. She informed me that the staff knew this was "her time." Still, on several occasions, I observed teachers darting in and out to ask questions or just to say good morning. She took the "intrusions" in stride as she really did not mind.

There were many piles of papers on Ms. Marshall's desk. In addition there were several bookshelves around the office containing various curriculum materials. She also had several plants in her office and a few simple artifacts hanging on the wall.

During my fall 1984 visit, Ms. Marshall spent about 75 percent of her day out of her office. During my visits her typical day went something like the following:

7:25 arrival, putting on make-up

7:45 teacher in office for discussion

8:15 discussion with researcher

8:40 teacher in office for discussion

8:55 student and parent in for discipline problem

9:15 classroom observations

10:15 discussion with custodial engineer in hall

10:25 in staff lounge talking with teachers

11:00 talking with teacher in hall

11:10 back to office to place call

11:20 miscellaneous desk work in office

11:55 to nurse's office to check on sick student

12:05 discussion with teacher in hall

12:15 to lunch in staff lounge

1:00 meeting in office with parent, regarding discipline

1:25 discussion with researcher

1:50 teacher in office for request

2:10 phone call placed

2:20 husband in to discuss personal matters

2:35 discussion with parent regarding discipline

3:00 discussion with student regarding discipline

3:20 teacher in to discuss classroom lessons

3:35 discussion with researcher

4:00 discussion in hall with office manager

4:10 discussion with parent and student

4:30 discussion with office manager in hall

4:35 departure

Ms. Marshall's schedule shifted somewhat during my winter 1985 visit. She explained that when I came to Woodson in the fall, she had three new teachers and had to spend a large amount of time observing and meeting with them. In the winter, things had settled down, her expectations were clear to the new teachers, and observations were less frequent. She did not observe at all during my second visit. One veteran teacher told me that Ms. Marshall observes her class, with notice, twice a year.

CARTER G. FOSTER ELEMENTARY SCHOOL

Setting

Carter G. Foster is located in a central California city of 150,000 with a mixed population of apartment dwellers and homeowners. The school is in the Kumasi Unified School District.

Foster was built in 1972. There were four portable classrooms. On the wall in the all-purpose room there were large posters of Booker T. Washington, Frederick Douglass, George Washington Carver, W. E. B. DuBois, and Duke Ellington.

Teachers

There were fourteen teachers at Foster with an average of fifteen years of total teaching experience. The average teacher had been there since 1978. There were ten white teachers and four African-American teachers. All of the nonteaching staff were African-American or Hispanic. Teachers seemed to cluster in groups by race at Foster. In the cafeteria, for example, white teachers sat primarily with white teachers and African-Americans tended to stay together. Despite this selective seating, all staff seemed to work together well. Teacher attitudes were typified by this comment from one teacher:

I think we have a very friendly faculty and administration. I think we all feel comfortable together. So I think that has a lot to do with the general morale.

I don't think there's a big black/white feeling around this school at all among the faculty socially. We all socialize and do a lot of things together. So I think it's a really comfortable situation.

Students

The student population at Foster was 66 percent African-American, 26 percent Hispanic, and 8 percent Asian. The 380 students at Foster represented a considerably lower number than the district elementary school average of 620.

In the midst of a poverty-stricken community, the children at Foster previously had to flash identifying cards to show that they were eligible for free lunch. During the 1984–85 academic year, the number of eligible children had swelled to such a high level (98 percent) that the decision was made by the district to discontinue the use of the cards and admit all students to the free lunch program.

Parents

Only about ten parents came to PTA meetings at Foster. However, at school programs such as open school nights and back-to-school nights the average number of parents was "much higher" according to the principal.

Of the dozen or so parents who volunteered at Foster, most were parents of kindergarten students. Typical tasks included classroom assistance and chaperoning field trips. Only four of the paid aides at Foster were parents of students at the school. Over 50 percent of the students lived in single-parent homes, where their parents were usually underemployed or unemployed.

The staff at Foster made a point to encourage parents to participate. While I observed, on several occasions parents came into the principal's office for reasons other than student discipline. In one instance, a parent visited the principal to discuss the lack of involvement of other parents. On another occasion, a parent was concerned about supervision on an upcoming field trip. I also saw parents talking with teachers in classrooms after school. One teacher told me that a white principal in the district had said that, in his mind, the area surrounding Foster is a "real community" with very responsive parents.

Principal

Harold Brooks, the principal at Foster, was a man in his mid-fifties with an M.A. in educational administration. In the words of one teacher, "he knows [the] . . . community probably better than anybody in town in any type of business field." This thought was echoed by many teachers at Foster. Mr. Brooks was more active in the larger community than the other two principals. For instance, during my fall visit, community meetings were being held in an attempt to get a middle school in the community so students would no longer have to be bused. Mr. Brooks attended all of these meetings and played an active role. He had served on the Juvenille Justice Commission in the city for one year, had been a member of the city's Redevelopment Agency for four years, and was in his eighth year on the planning commission. He also had been involved in several organizations in his immediate community including an African-American men's group and an African-American educators' group for which he once served as president.

He taught on the elementary level for ten years before becoming a principal in 1963. From 1963 to 1967 he served as the principal of two schools simultaneously. From 1967 to 1972 he was the principal in two others for a total of five years before coming to Foster. Mr. Brooks had chosen to remain at Foster despite numerous and continual offers from the district to move him to other schools.

The staff at Foster agreed that Mr. Brooks was somewhat low key but that he combined an even temper and a strong commitment to the education of the children at Foster. When asked to identify what sets Foster apart from other schools, everyone pointed first to Mr. Brooks's personal qualities.

On Mr. Brooks's daily rounds during my visits, he would note minor imperfections in the otherwise very attractive facility. For example, on one yellow wall outside of the building, rain had apparently run down from the roof in a straight line and left a dark residue on the wall. He was very concerned about having that darkened area cleaned up. He would often examine the contents of the lunch area garbage cans to see what the children tended to throw away and, conversely, which foods they seemed to like.

Mr. Brooks's routine did not change at all for my two visits. He followed the same basic routine each day. Typically he would arrive at 7:30 A.M. and remain until around 4:30 P.M.:

7:30 observing kindergarten class

7:40 to student breakfast area to observe

7:50 to office for discipline problem

8:15 on yard duty

8:40 to office to take phone call

8:45 classroom observations

9:50 to office to take a phone call and to place another one

10:00 conference with teacher

10:20 on break in lounge; informal discussions with teachers and researcher

10:35 to office to place a phone call

10:45 conference with teacher

11:05 office work and talking with researcher

11:30 parent in to discuss child's behavior

11:50 spontaneous socializing with custodial staff member

12:05 to children's eating area to observe

12:20 on yard duty

12:45 to lunch with researcher and teachers in lounge

1:35 parent in to discuss child's behavior

2:00 conference with teacher

2:20 outside observing dismissal, street crossing, and bus loading

2:40 disciplinary discussion with student

3:00 conference with teacher

3:20 placing calls

3:45 talking with researcher and doing desk work

4:30 departure

In discussing Mr. Brooks's attitude toward the children at Foster, one teacher said, "Number one with him is making the kids feel like they're really important and he tries to make sure they feel comfortable."

SUMMARY

In some ways, these three principals and their schools are similar (see table 5.2 for a synopsis of the similarities and differences). Total teacher experience in each school averages about fifteen years. Also, the principals each have ten or more years of teaching experience and nine or more years of administrative experience. The length of the principal's day in each school is also similar. Mr. Brooks and Ms. Marshall spend about nine hours at their schools each day, while Mr. Charles spends about eight hours. With regard to students, all of the schools have 80 percent or more of their children receiving free lunches.

Several differences in these principals and their schools are also apparent. While Collins and Woodson are both in large, urban areas, Foster is located in a much smaller city. Different housing patterns are found surrounding each of the schools—Collins, private homes; Woodson, apartments; and Foster, homes and apartments.

In each school the average teacher has served at least three years. Teacher tenure at Foster averages six years; teacher tenure is at the lowest level at Collins (average of three years). Woodson is the only school in which the staff chooses to sit in the lounge without regard to race.

Woodson is the only school of the three with a primarily African-American teaching staff (60 percent African-American). In both Collins and Foster most teachers are white. In Collins, whites make up 75 percent and at Foster they represent 67 percent of the faculty.

Collins has the highest percentage of African-American students (85 percent). African-American students at both Woodson and Foster make up about two-thirds of the student

Table 5.2
Summary of Components of Schools in Sample

		COLLINS	WOODSON	FOSTER
I.	Setting			
	a. city	large, urban	large, urban	medium,
	b. Housing	private homes	apartments	semi-rural homes/ apartments
II.	Teachers			
	a. average tenure at school (in years)	3	4	6
	b. average total tenure	14 years	15 years	15 years
	c. % of new teachers	48	19	36
	d. largest racial group (%)	75 (White)	60 (Black)	67 (White)
	e. total number	23	27	14
	f. staff lounge racial arrangement	segregated	integrated	segregated
III.	Students			
	a. % Black	85	65	66
	b. total number	581	798	387
	c. % with both parents in home	60	3	50
	d. % getting free lunch	83	80	100
IV.	Parents			
	a. average number at PTA meetings	30	not applicable	10
	b. number who volunteer	30	10	12
	c. % of aides who are parents	67	50	25
	d. do most work?	yes	yes	no
V.	Principal			
	a. distance to work (miles)	75	45	<10
	b. age	in 60s	in 40s	in 50s
	c. teaching exper. (in years)	16	13	10
	d. admin. exper. (in years)	15	9	21
	e. typical day	8 AM-4 PM	7:25 AM-4:35 PM	7:30 AM-4:30 P
	f. predominant activities during observations	talking with researcher in office; talking with researcher and coordinator in lounge; observing	talking with researcher; talking with individual teachers; observing; disciplinary problems	observing; doin office work; conferring with individual teachers

population. While half of the students in Collins and Foster live with both parents, less than one in forty students at Woodson lives with both parents.

Parent involvement is highest at Collins, where there is the highest average number of parents at PTA meetings (thirty), as well as the highest number of parents who volunteer (thirty). In addition, Collins has the highest percentage of aides who are also parents of students enrolled in the school (67 percent). All of the schools show a high level of contact between parents and teachers, while Collins was the only school without a high level of contact between parents and the principal.

Mr. Brooks, at Foster, is the only principal who lives relatively close to his school. Ms. Marshall and Mr. Charles both commute over forty miles.

There were some striking differences in the way each of the principals spent their time during my observations. Mr Charles' two most time-consuming activities were talking with the researcher in the office and talking with the researcher and the Title I coordinator in the staff lounge. Mr. Brooks was the only principal for whom observing ranked number one in terms of the amount of time spent participating in activities included in his daily routine.

NOTE

1. All names of schools, school districts, and principals are fictitious.

6

How African-American Principals Lead

INTRODUCTION

Data for this study support the widely held notion that leaders in more effective schools, and leaders in general, do not use any one style of leadership (Lightfoot, 1983; Drucker, 1967; Manasse, 1985). The qualities of a given leader in one more effective school may be very different from those of a leader in another more effective school. This premise appears to be true for African-American principals in African-American schools. In fact, while two of my subjects were very similar in their styles, the third principal, Mr. Charles, exhibited leadership in a very different way. As a consequence, I describe Ms. Marshall's and Mr. Brooks' leadership first, followed by a discussion of my findings regarding the leadership of Mr. Charles.

Interestingly, teachers at Mr. Charles' school were significantly more verbal in interviews and on questionnaires. Teacher interviews at Collins lasted, on an average, more than forty minutes, while at the other schools, they lasted approximately twenty minutes. There was a significantly larger number of teachers at Collins who voluntarily added comments on their questionnaires as well. This made it somewhat difficult to provide a balanced account of each school given the large difference in the amount of data collected and subsequently analyzed.

FOSTER ELEMENTARY SCHOOL

Goal Development

Types of Goals. In talking with Mr. Brooks, the principal at Foster, I learned that there are goals at Foster in the areas of academics, student behavior, and student self-worth. Some of the academic goals focus on specific growth objectives for the children in each class. They are developed by teachers in consultation with the principal. The student behavior goals are summarized in the following discipline rules which hang in each classroom at Foster:

Foster School Classroom Rules

Each student will:

1. keep all parts of body and objects to self
2. not disturb the learning environment
3. remain in seat unless given permission
4. be prompt and orderly
5. show respect for self and others

If I choose to break the rules, these will be the consequences:

1. verbal warning
2. counseling
3. parent contact
4. office

In addition to the goals that are developed at the school, other academic and nonacademic goals at Foster are developed at the district level (see table 6.1 for an example of some of these goals).

How Goals Are Set. The five teachers I interviewed at Foster generally agreed that Mr. Brooks played a key role in the development of the goals at Foster. One teacher said, "Our goals are discussed at the beginning of the year. Mr. [Brooks] brings up a

Table 6.1
Sample Goals—Foster Elementary School (1983–84)

I. By June 1984, Foster students CAT reading median grade scores should be no less than:

Grade	Score
K	70%
1	1.9
2	2.9
3	3.9
4	4.9
5	5.9
6	6.9

II. By May 1984, students who have been in attendance prior to October 15th (excluding those who have missed 10 school days) median scores will be at grade level or above as evidenced by the result of CAT scores administered in May 1984.

III. By June 1984, K-3 Foster students will develop a greater awareness of various cultures and/or individuals within those cultures as measured by teacher assessment or observation.

IV. By June 1984, all K-2 students will be screened, diagnosed as verified by the speech therapist's records (district speech language and hearing therapy program will be maintained.

V. By June 1984, the Foster library clerk will perform the duties outlined in major solutions procedures as verified by principal's observation of pertinent records on file in the school library.

subject for discussion and the staff brainstorms and decides on a policy." Another teacher told me that Mr. Brooks's role is low key in this process, as he lets teachers take the lead. Still another teacher added that Mr. Brooks's role in goal development is one of "guidance."

According to teacher responses on the questionnaire, the goals at Foster are often framed with responsibilities and are easily translatable into classroom objectives. On the questionnaire, Mr. Brooks's mean scores for these questions were 4.5 and 4.3, respectively (see table 6.2, questions 2 and 3; the reader will recall that scores on the questionnaire ranged from 1 [almost never] to 5 [almost always]. Also, in coding, I considered a principal to possess a particular quality if the mean score was above 3.9). The formulation of easily translatable goals is a major aspect of the goal development variable.

Table 6.2
Teacher Responses on Questionnaire—Foster Elementary School—Goal Development

	MEAN	STANDARD DEVIATION	N
1. Frames the school's goals with target dates	4.1	1.1	10
2. Frames the school's goals in terms of staff responsibilities for meeting them	4.5	0.7	10
3. Develops goals that are easily translatable into classroom objectives by teachers	4.3	0.7	10
4. Develops goals that seek improvement over current levels of performance	4.3	0.9	10
5. Uses data on student performance when developing the school academic goals	4.8	0.8	9
AREA OVERALL MEAN	4.4		

Note: The following is the key for the mean scores:

1 = almost never
2 = seldom
3 = sometimes
4 = frequently
5 = almost always

Mr. Brooks is intimately involved in the development of all of the goals that are developed at Foster. These goals are provided for teachers in a staff handbook. Mr. Brooks told me that his involvement includes participation in meetings at which goals are developed. He serves as a guide in this process.

Generally, during my observations it was clear that Mr. Brooks took the goals at Foster seriously. Much of his activity was related to the institutional goals. For example, on several occasions I heard him talking with teachers and students about the need to focus on the development of positive self-concepts in all of the students.

Energy Harnessing

Staff Cooperation. One teacher at Foster emphasized that Mr. Brooks is task-oriented and, accordingly, brings teachers together to focus on specific tasks when necessary. The kind of relationships that he has developed with his staff are such that they are generally receptive to his requests and suggestions. This receptivity does not, however, border on autocracy; the teachers feel free to disagree and they believe that their views are taken seriously.

The staff at Foster works harmoniously and cooperatively. In the staff lounge there is often a chattering among the teachers on nearly any topic, including academics, social life, or family life. I recall, during my observations, only positive discussions about students or about teaching responsibilities. These observations are important because this warm environment appears to contribute to Mr. Brooks's ability to encourage teachers to support the school goals. In addition, in a warm, supportive environment teachers are more willing to work toward the goals. This is particularly true when the principal provides the kind of leadership that is conducive to facilitating this goal-oriented work. The fact that Mr. Brooks frequently has the support of key teachers in his school, as indicated by the mean score of 4.5 on the teacher questionnaire, is important also (see table 6.3, question 2).

Energy-Harnessing Methods. Some of Mr. Brooks's methods of energy harnessing, according to the responses I received during the teacher interviews, have been discussions in staff meetings, demonstrations, recommending college classes to teachers, new teacher orientation, individual conferences, and calling in specialists in various areas.

According to teacher responses on the questionnaire, Mr. Brooks is aware of the various personalities of the teachers,

Table 6.3

Teacher Responses on Questionnaire—Foster Elementary School—Energy Harnessing

	MEAN	STANDARD DEVIATION	N
1. Keeps staff working together as a team	4.1	0.8	11
2. Has support of key teachers/ teacher group	4.5	0.8	11
3. Distributes notes, announcements, or newsletters to teachers informing them of opportunities for professional development that are related to the school's goals	4.5	0.7	10
4. Selects in-service activities that are consistent with the school's academic goals	4.5	0.5	10
5. Distributes journal articles to teachers on a regular basis	3.6	1.3	11
6. Ensures that instructional aides receive appropriate training to help students meet instructional objectives	3.2	0.9	10
7. Arranges for outside speakers to make presentations on instructional issues at faculty meetings	3.8	0.8	10
8. Provides time to meet individually with teachers to discuss instructional issues	4.0	1.1	11
AREA OVERALL MEAN	4.2		

listens to them, considers their personal welfare, and is friendly and approachable. His mean scores on the questionnaire in these areas were 4.5, 4.9, 4.7, and 4.8, respectively. Teachers at Foster feel that Mr. Brooks almost always exhibits these qualities (see table 6.4, questions 8, 10, 11, and 12). Though these questions are in the section of the questionnaire that is related to communication facilitation, it appears as though these qualities also contribute to Mr. Brooks's ability to harness the energy of his staff.

Teachers also indicated on the questionnaire that once Mr. Brooks hires teachers he regularly distributes professional development literature. His mean score was 4.5 on this question. That is, teachers felt that he almost always distributes such literature (see table 6.3, question 3). Mr. Brooks usually selects in-service topics that are consistent with efforts toward achieving the school's goals and that focus directly on these goals. His mean score was also 4.5 on this question in the questionnaire (see table 6.3, question 4). Mr. Brooks told me that he regularly provides these in-service programs in an attempt to further familiarize new staff with the school philosophy.

Individual principal/teacher conferences occur almost daily at Foster. I observed several such conferences, and teachers emphasized the significance of the sessions in the teacher interviews. These unusually regular, informal meetings, sometimes called by a teacher and sometimes called by Mr. Brooks, often emphasize bringing a teacher's classroom techniques in line with the school goals. It is through this and other tactics that Mr. Brooks quietly achieves a consensus around the goals as a first step toward directing the collective energy of his staff.

Mr. Brooks was about to hire a teacher while I was observing at Foster. He worked hard to check the backgrounds of the candidates and to ask them very specific questions during their interviews. He wanted to hire someone who was most in line with the philosophy of the school, thereby minimizing his efforts at achieving a consensus on the school's goals.

Table 6.4
Teacher Responses on Questionnaire—Foster Elementary School—Communication Facilitation

	MEAN	STANDARD DEVIATION	N
1. Refers to school goals in formal settings with teachers	4.0	0.5	10
2. Refers to school goals at faculty meetings	4.3	0.8	10
3. Refers to school goals when making curricular decisions with teachers	4.3	0.9	10
4. Ensures that the school goals are reflected in highly visible displays in the school (e.g., posters and bulletin boards) indicating the importance of reading and/or math	3.9	1.0	10
5. Refers to school goals in assemblies	3.7	1.1	10
6. Keeps staff well informed	3.9	0.7	11
7. Is easy to understand	4.6	0.7	10
8. Is generally knowledgeable of staff responsibilities, problems, and interests	4.5	0.5	11
9. Uses needs assessment or other questionnaire to secure staff input on goal development	4.2	0.9	10
10. Finds time to listen to staff members	4.9	0.3	11
11. Looks out for personal welfare of individual staff members	4.7	0.5	11
12. Is friendly and approachable	4.8	0.4	11
13. Makes staff members feel at ease when talking to them	4.4	0.8	11
AREA OVERALL MEAN	4.3		

There was a new teacher at Foster when I visited in the winter. Much of Mr. Brooks's energy at this time was spent on orienting this teacher to the school, all the while focusing on the school's goals and on the need for a team effort in order to achieve those goals.

Communication Facilitation

Frequency and Amount of Communication. In discussing the amount and frequency of communication, one teacher said, "He's [Mr. Brooks] very up front as far as what needs to take place as far as your curriculum. It's always short. It's always sweet. It's always to the point."

There were six questions on the teacher questionnaire related to the amount of communication from the principal to the teachers. Mr. Brooks's mean score was 3.9 or better on each question, suggesting that teachers perceived that he communicated frequently (see table 6.4, questions 1–4, 6, and 7).

Mr. Brooks communicates with teachers on a daily basis. Based upon my observations, one area of emphasis at Foster is time on task—specifically academic learning time. On several occasions I observed Mr. Brooks making it clear to teachers in discussions that time on task is an area to be focused on. Toward this end, he encouraged teachers to send disruptive children to the office and to take other necessary steps to allow for the allotted time on instruction. Based upon my observations at this school, the principal emphasizes the school goals on a daily basis.

Medium of Communication. According to Mr. Brooks, he communicates to his faculty primarily at staff meetings, during in-service programs, and in private sessions. These private conferences (mostly informal) between the principal and teachers regarding curriculum and teacher performance are usually in Mr. Brooks's office, but sometimes they occur in the staff lounge, in the hall, or in the yard. Typically they last anywhere from five to thirty minutes.

Feedback from Teachers. Based on teacher interviews, the large majority of the teachers at Foster feel comfortable offering feedback to Mr. Brooks. One teacher told me:

I think most of the teachers probably feel free to do it [offer feedback] in a faculty meeting and if they don't [feel comfortable doing it] there, I think most of them would feel free to talk with him individually.

This statement was representative of the feelings of all but one of the teachers I talked with. Mr. Brooks has made most teachers feel very comfortable approaching him on school-related matters.

One dissenting teacher (still somewhat bitter, by her own admission, from the procedure used to make an administrative reorganization decision last year which affected her personally) said that she felt uncomfortable offering feedback to Mr. Brooks and that she did not think others felt comfortable either.

Teachers indicated on the questionnaire that Mr. Brooks almost always finds time to listen to staff. His mean score was 4.9 in this area. Teachers also said that he frequently makes them feel at ease when he talks with them. His mean score on this question was 4.4 (see table 6.4, questions 10 and 13).

During our interview, Mr. Brooks told me, "I have an open door policy. I'm never too busy to talk with teachers." My observations of Mr. Brooks's behavior and of the way teachers seemed to feel comfortable approaching him supported the belief that an actual open door policy does exist. Mr. Brooks appears to make a sincere effort to encourage teachers to offer feedback to him on school-related matters. It was rare, during my observations, that Mr. Brooks left the building. There was an implicit focus, on his part, on being available to teachers.

Instructional Management: Curriculum Planning

Involvement by the principal in curriculum planning is one aspect of instructional management. Most of the curriculum planning and development for Foster is handled on the district level.

When asked about Mr. Brooks's role in curriculum planning, one teacher said:

He's right there. He's right there to ask questions. We're supposed to come up with the questions and he's always been there at all the meetings when we've had to write the program.

Another teacher added:

[Sally, the curriculum specialist] does that with him [Mr. Brooks] and we sit down in meetings and plan and change the guidelines and check the data when the test results come out to see what we can do.

Teachers also indicated on the questionnaire, with a mean score of 4.2, that Mr. Brooks participates in curriculum review and selection meetings. They also noted, with a mean score of 4.5, that Mr. Brooks makes an effort to see that the texts used in the school are consistent with the academic goals (see table 6.5, questions 2 and 5).

Mr. Brooks told me that he does meet with staff for the planning that occurs on the school level. His role in curriculum planning includes active participation in planning meetings and providing curriculum ideas and materials for teachers. Though there is a person assigned to curriculum at Foster, Mr. Brooks directs all activities. On several occasions, I observed him discussing with this specialist the appropriate texts and placement of students.

Mr. Brooks also appeared to make an effort to stay abreast of new developments in curriculum. There were many materials in his office, such as journals, catalogues, and new texts, which suggested a keen interest in staying informed about new ideas in curriculum development.

Instructional Management: Teacher Supervision[1]

Frequency and Amount of Observation. In discussing Mr. Brooks's visibility as a supervisor, one teacher said:

Table 6.5
Teacher Responses on Questionnaire—Foster Elementary School—
Instructional Management (Curriculum Planning)

	MEAN	STANDARD DEVIATION	N
1. Makes clear to teachers who is responsible for coordinating curriculum content across grade levels (e.g. the principal, the vice-principal or a teacher)	4.2	1.1	11
2. Participates in meetings for the purpose of reviewing or selecting instructional materials	4.2	0.9	10
3. Ensures that the academic goals of the school are translated into common curricular objectives	4.4	1.0	10
4. Draws upon the results of schoolwide testing when making curricular decisions	4.6	0.8	10
5. Ensures that the content selected from textbooks by teachers is aligned with the school's curricular goals	4.5	0.5	10
OVERALL MEAN	4.3		

We have one [principal] that's very visible at all times. You've followed him around. He's usually around like that all the time—in and out of the rooms. One day last year, I counted. He was in my room six times. I mean actually six times during the day. He usually comes in at least once every day, in everybody's classroom.

Another teacher said, "He's in and out of the classes a lot, which, I think, has an effect on everyone's behavior."

In discussing his procedure for classroom observations, Mr. Brooks said:

I make classroom observations and we usually have a rating sheet that we will [use to] score them on their performance on that particular area and we will meet with them after the observation and go over what we observed and offer suggestions for improvement. So, in our area of reading, for instance, we have a certain form that I use—and we have one that's very similar for math and I have a form of this nature that I use for the other subjects.[2]

My observations confirmed that Mr. Brooks conducts classroom observations on a daily basis. Despite his regular attendance in classes, there was no indication of any resentment from teachers. His visits appeared to be welcome.

Nature of Principal Feedback. Mr. Brooks provides written feedback on the classroom observations to at least one teacher each day. (See appendix G for a copy of the Kumasi Greater Achievement Program Evaluation Form).

Perhaps teacher supervision is the area of instructional management in which Mr. Brooks is strongest. Not only are his observations conducted on a daily basis, but there is written feedback and consultations with the teachers involved as deemed necessary. The responses of teachers during the interviews supported the view that this observation, feedback, and consultation occurs regularly. I observed Mr. Brooks providing the feedback and talking with teachers as a follow-up.

Instructional Management: Evaluation of Student Achievement

Nature of Principal Involvement. When discussing the way Mr. Brooks participates in the evaluation of academic achievement, one teacher said:

At the beginning of the year Mr. [Brooks] likes us to write our yearlong objectives. And then he will just sit down with you and evaluate your CAP scores with you at the end of the year. We just take them one at a time, in May, and we will look at each child's growth as determined in the objective—whether they're below that or above it.

But he's very supportive and it's a very low-key evaluation session, which is good. I really believe in that approach.

Table 6.6

Teacher Responses on Questionnaire—Foster Elementary School—Instructional Management (Evaluation of Student Achievement)

	MEAN	STANDARD DEVIATION	N
1. Assesses agreement between school's curricular goals and the achievement test(s) used for program evaluation	4.7	0.9	9
2. Meets individually with teachers to discuss pupil academic performance	4.2	0.8	11
3. Discusses the item analysis of schoolwide tests such as the CAP with the faculty in order to identify strengths and weaknesses in the school's instructional program	4.3	1.0	9
4. Uses the results of schoolwide testing to assess progress toward school academic goals	4.7	0.9	10
5. Distributes the results of student testing to teachers in a timely fashion	4.9	0.6	10
6. Informs teachers of the school's performance results on tests in written form (e.g., in memos or newsletters)	4.5	0.5	10
7. Informs students of the school's performance results	3.3	1.5	9
8. Identifies students whose performance on school tests indicates the need for special instruction or enrichment	3.9	1.5	9
9. Develops or finds the appropriate instructional program for students whose performance on tests indicates a need	4.0	1.2	9
OVERALL MEAN	4.2		

In teacher questionnaires, teachers indicated that Mr. Brooks consistently assures agreement between the school's goals and the testing instruments and uses the results of tests to assess progress toward the school's academic goals. His mean scores on these questions were 4.7 and 4.7 (see table 6.6, questions 1 and 4). Other questionnaire responses indicated that he discusses the test results with teachers and distributes the standardized test results to teachers. His mean scores were 4.3 and 4.9 in these areas, respectively. Teachers also indicated, on the questionnaire, with a mean score of 4.5, that he almost always distributes results in writing (see table 6.6, questions 3 and 5).

In discussing the evaluation of student achievement, Mr. Brooks told me that he is involved with teachers primarily as a consultant/guide in meetings where they discuss test results. Occasionally he meets with individual teachers to focus on the results for their particular class.

SUMMARY

There are written goals at Foster. Most academic goals are handed down from the district. Some academic goals, student behavior goals, and student self-worth goals are developed at the school. The locally developed goals, which Mr. Brooks is involved in developing, are easily translatable. There is a direct focus, by Mr. Brooks, on goal development. He provides assertive leadership in this area.

The staff at Foster works well together. Mr. Brooks uses several methods to ensure that teachers perform according to the school's objectives. Such methods include offering classroom demonstrations, staff meeting discussions, individual and small group conferences, new staff orientation, and classroom observations. These methods enable him to achieve a consensus on school goals as he encourages teachers to work together toward these goals.

Through staff meetings and in-service programs, Mr. Brooks stresses the school's goals and policies to staff. Frequent communication occurs among the staff at Foster, in large part because of the leadership of Mr. Brooks. Most teachers feel comfortable offering feedback to Mr. Brooks in any given area of the school's operation.

In the area of instructional management, Mr. Brooks serves as a guide for the staff. While much of the curriculum planning for Foster is done at the district level, for that which is done at the school, he is very involved, primarily by consulting with the curriculum specialist and attending curriculum-planning meetings. In addition, as an active leader in curriculum planning, Mr. Brooks seems to stay on top of new curriculum developments.

As a supervisor, Mr. Brooks, on a daily basis, conducts classroom observations. In addition, he offers written, and sometimes verbal, feedback to teachers based upon these observations. In the area of achievement evaluation, he does monitor schoolwide tests, reporting the results to teachers and students, Finally, he makes sure that an on-going alignment between curricular goals and the instructional program exists.

NOTES

1. There are no questions on the questionnaire related directly to the area of teacher supervision. I relied upon teacher interviews, principal interviews, and direct observation for data in this area.

2. Though Mr. Brooks often used the term "we" in describing this process, all my data indicated that the appropriate pronoun was "I," based on an assessment of who actually took the action.

REFERENCES

Drucker, P. F. 1967. *The Effective Executive*. London: Pan.
Lightfoot, S. L. 1983. *The Good High School*. New York: Basic.
Manasse, A. L. 1985. "Improving conditions for principal effectiveness: Policy implications of research." *Elementary School Journal* 85, no. 3: 439–63.

7

Woodson Elementary School

GOAL DEVELOPMENT

Types of Goals

There are written academic goals at Woodson that are developed at the district level (see table 7.1 for a sample of these goals). Goals in the areas of student behavior, parent participation, school climate, school beautification, and community outreach are developed at Woodson.

How Goals Are Set

In discussing the goal development procedure at Woodson, one teacher aptly characterized the style of the principal as "participatory management," where she brainstorms alternative solutions to problems, allowing teachers to discuss them and to make recommendations.

Teachers indicated on the questionnaires that Ms. Marshall frames goals with dates and with individuals who are to be responsible. She scored 4.5 and 4.6 on these questions (see table 7.2, questions 1 and 2). The teachers added that Ms. Marshall develops easily translatable goals (4.6) and goals that seek improvement in the school program (4.6) (see table 7.2, questions 3 and 4).

Table 7.1

Sample Goals—Woodson Elementary School (1984–85)

I. Kindergarten - Math

Place Value: Number System

Counts to 20
Recognizes numerals 1-12
Writes numerals 1-12
Knows number sequence 1-12, ex. 5, 6 _, 8, _

II. Second Grade - Math

Multiplication and Division
Knows multiplication facts through 5's

III. Kindergarten - Reading

1st Quarter

Follow simple oral direction
Recognize and write own name - first and last
Identify objects that are alike/different
Recognize left to right movement in reading
Understand top/bottom concept in reading

IV. Fourth Grade - Reading

3rd Quarter

Recognize and use regular plurals (f/fs, fe, ves, f/ves)
Choose correct action word form to go with "he" or "she"
Use context clues to determine meaning of word
Identify fact or opinion story
Tell main idea of story in own words
Identify cause and effect in story (oral/written)
Draw conclusions/predict outcomes from story context

Ms. Marshall told me that she is involved with teachers in the formulation of many of the school's goals. She emphasizes staff involvement in the development of many of these goals, especially those in the areas of academics, student behavior, and parent participation. Ms. Marshall also told me that the student behavior and parent involvement goals are developed by teachers. In these cases, teachers volunteer to meet in a group

Table 7.2
Teacher Responses on Questionnaire—Woodson Elementary School—Goal Development

	MEAN	STANDARD DEVIATION	N
1. Frames the school's goals with target dates	4.5	0.7	16
2. Frames the school's goals in terms of staff responsibilities for meeting them	4.6	0.6	16
3. Develops goals that are easily translatable into classroom objectives by teachers	4.6	0.6	16
4. Develops goals that seek improvement over current levels of performance	4.6	0.6	16
5. Uses data on student performance	4.7	0.6	15
AREA OVERALL MEAN	4.6		

to discuss and plan goals. They then distribute their recommendations to the entire staff for feedback. Still other goals are developed by students (in areas such as school climate and school beautification) through the student council, according to Ms. Marshall. As a part of her responsibility to the district, Ms. Marshall also prepares annual school goals in the areas of school climate and community outreach.

ENERGY HARNESSING

Staff Cooperation

A newer teacher at Woodson emphasized that the staff there is "like a family." She said they work together often and that their personal relationships often extend beyond the school. This family concept is consistent with Selznick's notion of institutionalization. He suggests that in such a situation a certain climate permeates an organization and influences all the staff.

In discussing the way new teachers are affected by the strong influence of older teachers and by the leadership of the principal, one teacher said:

The ones, maybe, that she had a problem with, maybe they're in line now because most of us are old people here, you know, old teachers. I don't mean age-wise, but I mean we've been here a couple of years or a few years, so if there's been any problem, they kinda fall into line, and once you see other teachers doing, it's kinda hard for you not to do.

Here again, the effect of the school's climate is suggested. Teachers are influenced by the behavior of their peers to accept school norms and to participate cooperatively in striving for institutional goals.

One veteran teacher told me that Ms. Marshall's fairness in dealing with staff encourages teachers to adhere to institutional goals. An important factor in energy harnessing is a perception on the part of one's staff that the leader is being fair in his or her dealings with the staff.

The importance of fairness was supported by the teachers on the questionnaire where they indicated that Ms. Marshall almost always has their support. Her mean score in this area was 4.5 (see table 7.3, question 2).

Energy-Harnessing Methods

In this area the teachers I interviewed at Woodson agreed—Ms. Marshall does attempt to affect the behavior of teachers and is almost always effective. These efforts are geared toward staff agreement on school goals and the provision of the leadership necessary to move the staff forward in the quest of these goals.

Ms. Marshall told me that her energy-harnessing methods include defining appropriate behavior from the onset, staying in

Table 7.3
Teacher Responses on Questionnaire—Woodson Elementary School—Energy Harnessing

	MEAN	STANDARD DEVIATION	N
1. Keeps staff working together as a team	4.3	1.0	16
2. Has support of key teachers/ teacher groups	4.5	0.7	16
3. Distributes notes, announcements, or newsletters to teachers informing them of opportunities for professional development that are related to the school's goals	4.7	0.7	16
4. Selects in-service activities that are consistent with the school's academic goals	4.7	0.6	16
5. Distributes journal articles to teachers on regular basis	4.1	1.1	16
6. Ensures that instructional aides receive appropriate training to help students meet instructional objectives	4.3	0.9	13
7. Arranges for outside speakers to make presentations on instructional issues at faculty meetings	4.1	0.9	14
8. Provides time to meet individually with teachers to discuss instructional issues	4.4	1.1	16
AREA OVERALL MEAN	4.4		

touch with teachers on a daily basis, and arranging workshops with outside specialists. She went on to tell me that she sometimes urges teachers to take outside classes. Ms. Marshall provides classroom demonstrations for teachers. She pairs two teachers (one experienced and one new) for the sharing of ideas.

She also uses staff meetings, assemblies, and appropriate curriculum materials to rally her troops. If all else fails, Ms. Marshall will arrange for a teacher to be transferred to another
school.

In fact, Ms. Marshall's highest mean scores in this area on the
teacher questionnaire were for distributing professional
development materials to staff and selecting appropriate in-
service activities. Teachers felt that she almost always did these
two things (4.7) (see table 7.3, questions 3 and 4).

COMMUNICATION FACILITATION

Frequency and Amount of Communication

When asked to discuss how often Ms. Marshall communicates with teachers, one teachers aid:

She's very verbal, so she just tells you these are the goals that we want
to work on. Try to work on them in your classroom. Kids try to work on
them with each other. Try to work on them outside, just verbally. She'll
say in a staff meeting, these are the things that I want you to work
on—blank, blank, blank. And then, sometimes when we're having
lunch or we're just sitting down, she'll say, how's it going on this? Are
you working on that? Or either when she sees the kids outside walking
at lunch time—that kind of thing. So it's both—formally and informally.

The suggestion here is that Ms. Marshall focuses on emphasizing the goals throughout the day and can comfortably discuss
them with teachers and students in any setting.

Medium of Communication

The teachers at Woodson stated in the questionnaire that Ms.
Marshall refers to the goals in faculty meetings as well as in
curriculum meetings. Her mean scores were 4.4 and 4.6 on
these questions (see table 7.4, questions 2 and 3).

Ms. Marshall told me that additional communication vehicles she uses include individual discussions, assemblies,

Table 7.4

Teacher Responses on Questionnaire—Woodson Elementary School—Communication Facilitation

	MEAN	STANDARD DEVIATION	N
1. Refers to school goals in formal settings with teachers	4.4	0.8	16
2. Refers to school goals at faculty meetings	4.4	0.8	16
3. Refers to school goals when making curricular decisions with teachers	4.6	0.7	16
4. Ensures that the school goals are reflected in highly visible displays in the school (e.g., posters and bulletin boards) indicating the importance of reading and/or math	4.3	0.9	15
5. Refers to school goals in assemblies	4.1	1.0	16
6. Keeps staff well informed	4.4	1.0	14
7. Is easy to understand	4.2	1.3	16
8. Is generally knowledgeable of staff responsibilities, problems, and interests	4.3	1.0	15
9. Uses needs assessment or other questionnaire to secure staff input on goal development	4.4	0.9	16
10. Finds time to listen to staff members	4.5	0.8	15
11. Looks out for personal welfare of individual staff members	4.3	0.8	15
12. Is friendly and approachable	4.7	0.7	15
13. Makes staff members feel at ease when talking to them	4.7	0.6	16
AREA OVERALL MEAN	4.4		

PTA meetings, and back-to-school and open school nights.

Feedback from Teachers

At Woodson, the principal does solicit feedback from teachers on goals and policies. Ms. Marshall's teachers confirmed that she has an open door policy and that they do not feel at all threatened when approaching her regardless of the situation. With regard to the way Ms. Marshall might deal with a teacher's problem, one teacher said, "She's a no-nonsense person. She'll take care of it immediately." Another teacher said:

I think because [Ms. Marshall's] the type that you can walk in [on] any time and have a fairly easy relationship with, they're more apt to tell her, "I'm having problems with this and I can't do this. Can I do something else? The way that you told me to do it I can't do it, but I have another way. Do you mind if I do it my way?" They're free to walk in and talk about it and let her know. Or either we have grade-level chairmen. They can tell the grade-level [chairmen] and they'll transfer it to her.

Still another teacher said:

If we can't follow whatever the rules are, then we'll go in and have a discussion with the principal and she's always free to talk with [teachers]. She talks with us. We don't get pushed away or anything.

Teachers reiterated this notion of comfortableness in dealing with Ms. Marshall in their responses on the questionnaire. They felt that she did listen to staff, that she appeared friendly, and that she made them feel at ease. Her mean scores were 4.5, 4.7 and 4.7 on these questions (see table 7.4, questions 10, 12, and 13).

During my observations, teachers came to Ms. Marshall throughout the day to ask about, or to discuss, various curricular or noncurricular matters, lending support to the perceptions of these teachers.

INSTRUCTIONAL MANAGEMENT:
CURRICULUM PLANNING

Curriculum planning at Woodson is handled at the school level, primarily by grade-level representatives. The teachers I interviewed all agreed that Ms. Marshall's involvement was a vital ingredient in curriculum planning. She does participate in these meetings and generally stays abreast of new developments in the curriculum areas. One teacher said, "The curriculum coordinator and the principal work with teachers on curriculum planning."

Five teachers who were interviewed used ten words or phrases to describe Ms. Marshall's involvement in this area: "guide," "overseer," "facilitator," "idea-giver," "reinforcer," "involved," "consultant," "active," "experienced," and "advice-giver."

Ms. Marshall almost always helps to ensure that the school goals are translated into classroom objectives. Teachers indicated this on the questionnaire, where her mean score was 4.6 (see table 7.5, question 3).

Ms. Marshall's involvement in curriculum planning during my observations included regularly scheduled (and sometimes unscheduled) meetings with the staff person responsible for textbook acquisition. I observed two such meetings.

INSTRUCTIONAL MANAGEMENT:
TEACHER SUPERVISION

Frequency and Number of Observations

During an interview, one seasoned teacher told me that her class is generally observed by Ms. Marshall twice a year. However, Ms. Marshall spent most of her mornings observing teachers when I visited Woodson in the fall. All of these observations were with new teachers. She did not do any observing when I returned in the winter. She explained to me that the apparent discrepancy was due to the fact that she generally

Table 7.5
Teacher Responses on Questionnaire—Woodson Elementary
School—Instructional Management (Curriculum Planning)

	MEAN	STANDARD DEVIATION	N
1. Makes clear to teachers who is responsible for coordinating curriculum content across grade levels (e.g. the principal, the vice-principal, or a teacher)	4.3	0.8	16
2. Participates in meetings for the purpose of reviewing or selecting instructional materials	4.4	0.7	15
3. Ensures that the academic goals of the school are translated into common curricular objectives	4.6	0.6	16
4. Draws upon the results of schoolwide testing when making curricular decisions	4.4	0.7	13
5. Ensures that the content selected from textbooks by teachers is aligned with the school's curricular goals	4.3	0.8	15
OVERALL MEAN	4.3		

spends a lot of time observing and offering feedback to new teachers and spends considerably less time observing veteran teachers. My observations supported the view that Ms. Marshall focuses on classroom observations, particularly with new teachers at the beginning of the year.

Nature of Principal Feedback

Ms. Marshall attempts to quickly identify the strengths and weaknesses of new teachers so that she can provide them with whatever assistance is necessary to improve their teaching skills. Also, throughout the year, she asks teachers, informally

Table 7.6
Teacher Responses on Questionnaire—Woodson Elementary School—Instructional Management (Evaluation of Student Achievement)

	MEAN	STANDARD DEVIATION	N
1. Assesses agreement between school's curricular goals and the achievement test(s) used for program evaluation	4.5	0.8	14
2. Meets individually with teachers to discuss pupil academic performance	3.9	0.9	15
3. Discusses the item analysis of schoolwide tests such as the CAP with the faculty in order to identify strengths and weaknesses in the school's instructional program	4.4	0.7	15
4. Uses the results of schoolwide testing to assess progress toward school academic goals	4.5	0.6	15
5. Distributes the results of student testing to teachers in a timely fashion	4.6	0.6	16
6. Informs teachers of the school's performance results on tests in written form (e.g., in memos or newsletters)	4.5	0.8	15
7. Informs students of the school's performance results	4.2	1.1	15
8. Identifies students whose performance on school tests indicates the need for special instruction or enrichment	4.1	1.2	15
9. Develops or finds the appropriate instructional program for students whose performance on tests indicates a need	4.3	0.9	16
OVERALL MEAN	4.3		

and in meetings, to report on progress in the instructional programs in their classrooms.

INSTRUCTIONAL MANAGEMENT: EVALUATION OF STUDENT ACHIEVEMENT

Ms. Marshall told me that she meets with teachers to interpret the scores for purposes of diagnosis and placement and distributes the written results of standardized tests to teachers. Teachers confirmed these statements on the teacher questionnaire, giving Ms. Marshall mean scores of 4.4 and 4.5, respectively (see table 7.6, questions 3 and 6). Teachers also suggested that she relates these scores in a practical way to students and their needs (see table 7.6, questions 7–9).

Teachers and Ms. Marshall work together on achievement evaluation at Woodson. According to Ms. Marshall, once the scores are received at the school, she reviews them. Ms. Marshall also told me that teachers meet on a grade-level basis with her to make placement decisions.

SUMMARY

Woodson has written goals, some of which are developed by the entire staff. Other goals are developed either by teachers alone or in some cases by students. Ms. Marshall is directly involved in this process.

Energy-harnessing techniques used by Ms. Marshall with staff include providing curriculum materials, staying in touch on a daily basis, and being a role model. She appears to do well in rallying teachers around school goals and in leading them to work toward these goals.

Staff meetings, one-on-one meetings, and assemblies provide most of Ms. Marshall's opportunities to articulate the school's goals to her teachers. Feedback is not a problem for her staff. They feel free at all times to bring their concerns to her.

As an instructional manager, Ms. Marshall plays an important role in curriculum planning, in the evaluation of student achievement, and as a supervisor of teachers. She provides the leadership in seeing that tasks are completed in each of these areas.

8

Collins Elementary School

GOAL DEVELOPMENT

Types of Goals

There are written and unwritten goals, both academic and non-academic at Collins (see table 8.1 for a sample of the written goals). Collins receives both from the district and is also involved on a school level in developing both academic and nonacademic goals.

One veteran teacher told me, "This school is very well organized as far as goals are concerned and I've taught in many schools."

The unwritten goals include high test scores, strict discipline, and mutual respect. In talking about the way the unwritten goals are dealt with, one teacher said:

[These] goals are inferred. . . . The principal may imply in his meetings that he wants the children treated a certain way. He doesn't want the children to be called dumb or whatever. You have to use nice terms. He doesn't like teachers sitting and talking about children. So there's an inference there that the goal is a positive self-concept.

Teachers were clear on this in our lengthy discussions and Mr. Charles stated these goals to me. My observations indicated that Mr. Charles personally embodied these unwritten goals.

Table 8.1
Sample Goals—Collins Elementary School (1984–85)

I.   Collins will have on file a two-year plan to strengthen the total instructional program with available resources. The plan will have been developed with staff and parent input. Information regarding the two-year plan and its implementation will be shared with the school community.

II. Collins will maintain a program which provides recognition for individual student progress and exceptional achievement.

III. Collins will provide to students and parents information which will help in interpreting the district/classroom standards used for assigning marks.

IV. Collins will continue to provide a schedule which requires regularly assigned student homework based upon classroom instruction.

V.   Collins will organize a school Beautification Drive/Campaign emphasizing a clean campus. This drive/campaign will include displays of students' work and the development of at least one area on the school campus to focus on aesthetic beauty.

VI. Collins will distribute to parents materials developed by the district which emphasize the suggestions in the district-prepared document, "A Shared Responsibility."

How Goals Are Set

According to the teachers, the responsibility for overseeing the goal development process is delegated by Mr. Charles to the Chapter 1 coordinator who worked on this area with teachers.[1] In discussing Mr. Charles' leadership in this area, one teacher explained to me:

He's great at delegating. So he'll probably say, okay, Mary, sit down with the teachers and go over X, Y, and Z goals and Mr. Jones, you sit down with this group and do this. But it's not him [Mr. Charles].

Mr. Charles is apparently not involved in the formulation of the goals that are developed at the school. His mean scores for principal involvement in goal development were below 3.9 (see table 8.2, questions 1–5). Most teachers felt that he infrequently exhibited these behaviors.[2]

Table 8.2
Teacher Responses on Questionnaire—Collins Elementary School—Goal Development

	MEAN	STANDARD DEVIATION	N
1. Frames the school's goals with target dates	3.6	1.5	18
2. Frames the school's goals in terms of staff responsibilities for meeting them	3.8	1.5	17
3. Develops goals that are easily translatable into classroom objectives by teachers	3.4	1.5	17
4. Develops goals that seek improvement over current levels of performance	3.5	1.6	17
5. Uses data on student performance when developing the school academic goals	3.6	1.3	17
AREA OVERALL MEAN	3.6		

In spite of his lack of direct involvement in this area, Mr. Charles did explain to me the goal development procedure at Collins:

[It] was a joint venture between the administrative leadership and the staff. That is, classified and certificated, and the community, community leadership, and parents. We had some parent surveys and then, of course, there was a pupil survey and pupil participation in setting the goals. So we got involved in a three-way thing. Actually, the pupils are the most important.

ENERGY HARNESSING

Staff Cooperation

According to many teachers at Collins, based upon the interviews and the teacher questionnaire responses, Mr. Charles has

Table 8.3
Teacher Responses on Questionnaire—Collins Elementary
School—Energy Harnessing

	MEAN	STANDARD DEVIATION	N
1. Keeps staff working together as a team	2.9	1.5	16
2. Has support of key teachers/ teacher groups	3.1	1.4	16
3. Distributes notes, announcements, or newsletters to teachers informing them of opportunities for professional development that are related to the school's goals	3.1	1.6	16
4. Selects in-service activities that are consistent with the school's academic goals	3.3	1.3	16
5. Distributes journal articles to teachers on regular basis	2.5	1.6	15
6. Ensures that instructional aides receive appropriate training to help students meet instructional objectives	2.9	1.7	15
7. Arranges for outside speakers to make presentations on instructional issues at faculty meetings	3.0	1.5	16
8. Provides time to meet individually with teachers to discuss instructional issues	3.3	1.6	18
AREA OVERALL MEAN	3.1		

trouble relating to teachers. The teacher questionnaire responses indicated that he is not easy to understand (2.9) (see table 8.3, question 7). Despite the fact that this question appears on the questionnaire under communication facilitation, it is significant here because this problem severely limits Mr Charles' ability to pull people together in a productive working relationship. His overall average on the eight questions on the teacher questionnaire related to energy harnessing was 3.1. Teachers felt that he infrequently did the things shown on the questionnaire related to energy harnessing (see table 8.3, questions 1–8).

One teacher told me in an interview that the high teacher turn-over rate at Collins is attributable, in part, to Mr. Charles' interpersonal relationships. Another teacher said that Mr. Charles shows whom he likes and whom he does not. Still another teacher added that there are three groups of teachers at Collins: "those he likes, those that are so-so, and those he dislikes."

In explaining Mr. Charles' energy-harnessing techniques, one experienced teacher said that he does attempt to affect behavior. "He gets rid of them. Well, you, know, come next year those people don't seem to be here." she said.

A few teachers suggested, and my observations provided support, that Mr. Charles usually reserved his few positive comments for white teachers. I was told by another teacher that he had had, on several occasions, confrontations with African-American male teachers. There were none at Collins when I was there. Two teachers said that earlier in the year one had been hired and fired within a few weeks because he had questioned one of Mr. Charles' plans in a staff meeting.

On one occasion while I was observing at Collins, Mr. Charles and I were walking down the hall on the second floor. A class was coming up the stairs, returning from the yard. Several students began running down the hall toward their class. Mr. Charles called to them to go back and walk down the hall. (They must have been fifty feet down the hall.) Just then the teacher appeared from the stairway and began explaining that she was sorry but that it was her fault that the students were running. Before she could finish, Mr. Charles said, "I don't care whose fault it is. Nobody runs in my school." (He was still fifty feet from them.) Teachers told stories of other instances where Mr. Charles had made verbal attacks on teachers in front of their classes, in some cases, bringing the teachers to tears.

Two other occurrences that I observed warrant attention. During a schoolwide spelling bee in the auditorium, Mr. Charles approached two children who had been told by their teacher to stand in different corners, apparently for disciplinary reasons. He told them quietly to take their seats. On the way out, when the program was over, he told the responsible teacher she should never place children in the corner for any reason because it had negative psychological ramifications. He went on to say that it was a school rule and asked if she understood. She said that she had never heard of the rule. He responded that she had heard it now.

On another occasion, we were in Mr. Charles' office. Earlier in the day he had asked the coordinator to come to his office to discuss their reorganization plan. (The plan had been necessitated by the problem of overcrowded classes which was to be relieved by the addition of a new teacher within a week.) At several points during the conversation Mr. Charles had raised his voice. The coordinator was responding to his expressed desire to discuss reorganization. Mr. Charles had apparently decided, after telling her to come to his office, that it was too early to discuss the reorganization plan. By the end of the conversation, the coordinator was crying and had to leave. In leaving, the coordinator said, "I'm sorry I brought the reorganization material in." When she came in the next morning at about 8:15 to tell Mr. Charles about the upcoming 8:30 assembly, their interaction was as though the previous day's clash had never transpired.

Energy-Harnessing Methods

One teacher said of Mr. Charles' role in encouraging staff to conform: "He won't come directly. Now when he comes directly to you then that's after many conferences with others."

Mr. Charles told me that some of his energy-harnessing methods include in-service programs in areas such as classroom management and lesson-plan writing and meeting with teachers regarding lesson plans. With each of these techniques the responsibility is delegated. The in-service programs are handled by the coordinator or a resource teacher.

During our interview, Mr. Charles also told me:

We need to work with those strengths that people have. . . . When you focus too heavily on weak points, people get disgruntled [and] discouraged and they just aren't going to be as effective with children as they can be. One simple thing I try to do is treat the teachers as I would like to be treated in that room.

This statement, however, was inconsistent with much of what I observed and heard at Collins.

COMMUNICATION FACILITATION

Frequency and Amount of Communication

The teachers I interviewed at Collins agreed that Mr. Charles does regularly communicate the school's goals to teachers. One teacher told me, "Mr. [Charles] is pretty effective as far as making us aware of the goals. I think we all know what the goals are and I think he reiterates that many times during the year." Another teacher added:

Oh yes, we have our Monday morning assembly. We constantly have this. Well, Mr. [Charles] always gives a speech and it's, more or less, a reinforcement constantly. Sometimes it's about behavioral goals, sometimes it's instructional goals [and] sometimes it's just effective behavior, in general. But every week we get our reinforcement.

When asked how often Mr. Charles communicates goals to teachers, one teacher volunteered:

Every time he opens his mouth. All the time. He's always talking about the goals of the school and what we're trying to do. . . . Some of the

Table 8.4

Teacher Responses on Questionnaire—Collins Elementary School—Communication Facilitation

		MEAN	STANDARD DEVIATION	N
1.	Refers to school goals in formal settings with teachers	3.6	1.5	18
2.	Refers to school goals at faculty meetings	3.8	1.4	20
3.	Refers to school goals when making curricular decisions with teachers	3.5	1.5	17
4.	Ensures that the school goals are reflected in highly visible displays in the school (e.g., posters and bulletin boards) indicating the importance of reading and/or math	3.2	1.7	16
5.	Refers to school goals in assemblies	3.8	1.3	18
6.	Keeps staff well informed	3.1	1.4	17
7.	Is easy to understand	2.9	1.5	17
8.	Is generally knowledgeable of staff responsibilities, problems, and interests	2.8	1.7	15
9.	Uses needs assessment or other questionnaire to secure staff input on goal development	2.7	1.8	15
10.	Finds time to listen to staff members	3.5	1.7	17
11.	Looks out for personal welfare of individual staff members	3.4	1.7	17
12.	Is friendly and approachable	3.4	1.6	17
13.	Makes staff members feel at ease when talking to them	3.1	1.5	18
AREA OVERALL MEAN		3.3		

people that have been here for a while, they tend to turn him off. They say he goes on and on and on, but then if you're listening to what he's saying and can pick out some main ideas. He states them [goals] effectively by his talking on and on and on. That's the only way. He doesn't write. We don't get anything from him written. It's just in a meeting. . . .

She continued:

But because he does ramble, at times, on and on about different things, sometimes you don't know what he's talking about. Then when he finally gets to the point he's trying to make—he prefaces his point with a whole lot of conversation; that's the weakness in communication. But when he gets to what he wants to say, then you say, oh, okay, now what did he say before that. Now you gotta tie it all in. But other than that, it's verbal. He communicates to us in meetings.

Teacher questionnaire responses, however, showed that Mr. Charles did not frequently facilitate two-way communication. None of his thirteen mean scores in this area were above 3.8 (see table 8.4, questions 1–13).

Medium of Communication

Vehicles for communication include personal conferences, informal meetings, and assemblies. One experienced teacher said that the principal/teacher interactions at Collins were often of a negative nature. This teacher went on to say:

He browbeats and discourages an open line of communications. Perhaps that's why he delegates. It kind of turns you off. Rather than going and following through on the things that he's saying you . . . tend to draw back a little bit and not to follow through on it. It's difficult, sometimes, to separate the emotional from the rational. His ideas are good. It's just the method of presentation. Sometimes that's hard to take.

Feedback from Teachers

On this topic, one teacher said that Mr. Charles' attitude is that "there is a right way, a wrong way, and his way." A newer teacher told me:

It's not a "share an idea and let's discuss it" type of thing. The principal does it the way he feels it's best done and doesn't really listen to the reasons that teachers have for wanting to change things. He has unrealistic ways of doing things or things that aren't fitting the situation he just refuses to change. I'm not sure why. But it's not effective. I don't feel there's two-way communication of any sort. He tells us what to do and we need to do it.

Another teacher, responding to my question regarding the availability of adequate channels for teachers to offer feedback to Mr. Charles, said:

I think there are adequate channels, but nobody wants to communicate with him. You never want to get caught in there if you can avoid it, by any means. You never get caught in that office unless you have thirty to forty minutes, number one. You never do that. If it's something where—and then he gets upset, he can snap. He'll snap on you and go off and start ranting and raving. So you tend to avoid it. . . . So people turn off and they tend not to communicate with him at all because they don't want to go through that hassle. People don't want to go in that office. Don't get closed up in that office with him.

The teachers I interviewed at Collins told me that they rarely give feedback directly to Mr. Charles. From their perspective, the result would be a long drawn-out discussion probably highlighted by his yelling at them. Also, they do not feel that suggestions from teachers are taken seriously by Mr. Charles. When I asked one teacher if teachers offer feedback to Mr. Charles, she told me:

No. We're about peace here. If it's one [a suggestion] that you think he will accept, yes. But if it's one that you think will cause some disturbance simply because it's not in line with what he's stated, no.

You might go to the faculty chair or you might go to a resource person and if they can't work something out, then they'll go to him. We have a lot of mediators. That's how it works here. Some of us go to him, but most of the time it's through someone [else].

There was a consensus among the teachers—young and older, African-American and white, and new and veteran—that Mr. Charles was autocratic in communicating with staff. My observations supported this view.

In explaining his perspective on the issue of feedback from teachers on school goals, Mr. Charles told me:

In an elementary [school] you don't really have a lot of time for what you'd like to do in terms of meet and confer. It's . . . not enough. I'm an honest person. I would like to have more feedback, and I'd like to have more interchange, but we just don't have the time. In secondary [school], you have more time, because, you know, you have departmental meetings, but in elementary [school] you got this, here the teachers come in and they're with those kids all day except for lunch. You have a logistical problem.

Though Mr. Charles does attempt to communicate the goals to teachers, he does not personally encourage teachers to offer feedback but again delegates this authority.

INSTRUCTIONAL MANAGEMENT: CURRICULUM PLANNING

Much of the curriculum direction at Collins comes from the district. Any curriculum planning that does occur at Collins takes place in in-service programs and grade-level meetings. In this area the coordinator and resource teachers have the major coordination responsibilities. The role of Mr. Charles is minimal. There was a consensus among the teachers whom I interviewed that Mr. Charles is not directly involved in curriculum planning at Collins. A veteran teacher at Collins gave an indication as to why Mr. Charles' involvement in this area may be minimal:

I think Mr. [Charles] knows his stuff. There's absolutely no question about that. He knows the curriculum areas. He has his goals set. He knows where he wants to go. I just think he's very weak as far as getting teachers to work behind him and to pull with him and I think that the major reason is the lack of verbal communication skills.

Another teacher explained an instance in which Mr. Charles did exert his influence in the area of curriculum planning:

We have a new series in readers and the faculty wanted one set and the principal wanted another set. We got the set that he wanted. Well, after we looked at it, the set that he wanted was better.

The situation with the books was explained in a somewhat different way by another teacher:

I'm not exactly sure how much input we really had. I don't know if he was just going through the motions and had already decided on the program that he wanted because he was very strong in his remarks about the Ginn Reading Program. We knew that that was the program that he was in favor of. So, I think teachers kind of leaned in that direction but there was just as much support for the Macmillan as there was for Ginn.

Mr. Charles had a mean score below 3.8 on all of the questions on the teacher questionnaire which dealt with principal involvement in curriculum planning (see table 8.5, questions 1–5).

INSTRUCTIONAL MANAGEMENT: TEACHER SUPERVISION

Frequency and Number of Observations

Here again, Mr. Charles delegates much of his authority to the coordinator and resource teachers. He rarely observes classes. In discussing Mr. Charles' behavior regarding classroom observations at Collins, one teacher said:

Table 8.5
Teacher Responses on Questionnaire—Collins Elementary
School—Instructional Management (Curriculum Planning)

	MEAN	STANDARD DEVIATION	N
1. Makes clear to teachers who is responsible for coordinating curriculum content across grade levels (e.g. the principal, the vice-principal, or a teacher)	3.4	1.4	18
2. Participates in meetings for the purpose of reviewing or selecting instructional materials	3.1	1.7	16
3. Ensures that the academic goals of the school are translated into common curricular objectives	3.4	1.6	16
4. Draws upon the results of schoolwide testing when making curricular decisions	3.7	1.5	18
5. Ensures that the content selected from textbooks by teachers is aligned with the school's curricular goals	3.6	1.5	17
OVERALL MEAN	3.5		

He will possibly have his resource people come in and assist them [teachers] and he periodically gets into rooms to check lesson plans and maybe observe a lesson. He comes through for about ten minutes. This school year, today was the first day he came in when you were here. This is the first he's been in. Now he's been better in the past. He would usually have him or his resource teachers or his Chapter I person. He would have these people coming through quite a bit. . . . He doesn't do it that much any more.

Nature of Principal Feedback

My observations indicated that Mr. Charles usually leaves the responsibility of conferring with errant teachers to the coordinator. In explaining how Mr. Charles functions as a teacher supervisor, one experienced teacher said:

Probably by setting such a high standard for the school. We're the best school. We have to really impress everyone with the fact that we have these standards we're living up to. [Collins] School has always been top-notch. This kind of thing. So, I guess he gives you the feeling that if you're doing anything that's not quite center, why you're letting everyone down including the school and yourself. And I really have the feeling that he is an administrator that I respect. And I believe sincerely that you have to have a certain amount of—probably I don't know that fear is the word—but I do believe that he would replace me if I didn't do the right thing. I don't think I can push Mr. [Charles] around.

Another teacher said, "He makes sure that the teachers stay on their job. He fusses at you. He's like a father. . . . "

Mr. Charles, in discussing his perceptions of his role in staff supervision said:

My job, of course, is to try to spend as much time as I can in the classroom monitoring. Monitoring is the best thing. What I try to do with monitoring is, I try to really do a two-way thing—build up the strong points and help with the weak points—but you do them concurrently.

This statement was unconfirmed by what I saw and by what teachers reported.

INSTRUCTIONAL MANAGEMENT: EVALUATION OF STUDENT ACHIEVEMENT

Mr. Charles plays a minor role in the evaluation of achievement, according to the comments made by teachers during the interviews. One teacher said of Mr. Charles' role in this process: "It's a minimal role. It's pretty much left to the Chapter 1 coordinator, Ms. [Washington], and the teachers on the grade level." Another teacher added, "Scores on tests are looked at and analyzed by teachers and the coordinator and there is a supposition that there is follow-up in the class." When asked about Mr. Charles' role. this same teacher said, "He's pretty much out of it." A third teacher, describing the follow-up on test results at Collins, said:

In actuality, teachers basically deal with what they know, and what they observe in their classroom . . . this year. . . . We start out pre-testing . . . with the low skills or [the] high skills from the previous grade level. You have to assess yourself. Some of us kind of do that. So, therefore, the test scores mean nothing if you're gonna just go on your own. Then at the end of the year you might look at them [the scores]. Whenever we have to put up the lows, we'll look at the test scores . . . and say these are some areas we want to address but that's about it. We don't deal with them. We hear the next year we did well last year and that's it.

On the teacher questionnaire, none of Mr. Charles' mean scores on the nine questions related to principal involvement in the evaluation of student achievement exceeded 3.7. Again, based upon teacher perception, he infrequently displays these behaviors (see table 8.6, questions 1–9). He leaves the major responsibility in this area to the coordinator.

SUMMARY

Though there are written academic and nonacademic goals at Collins, Mr. Charles appears to play only a minor role in their development. Though he attempts to harness the energy of his staff, through such techniques as one-on-one meetings, Mr. Charles' interpersonal skills put him at a severe disadvantage in this area.

Mr. Charles communicates the school's goals to staff, although many people are offended by his presentation in such places as assemblies and staff meetings. He does not appear to provide direct input in the area of instructional leadership as defined in the literature on school effectiveness. He is only minimally involved in curriculum planning, the evaluation of student achievement, and teacher supervision.

Table 8.6

Teacher Responses on Questionnaire—Collins Elementary School—
Instructional Management (Evaluation of Student Achievement)

	MEAN	STANDARD DEVIATION	N
1. Assesses agreement between school's curricular goals and the achievement test(s) used for program evaluation	3.7	1.2	15
2. Meets individually with teachers to discuss pupil academic performance	2.9	1.7	14
3. Discusses the item analysis of schoolwide tests such as the CAP with the faculty in order to identify strengths and weaknesses in the school's instructional program	3.6	1.4	18
4. Uses the results of schoolwide testing to assess progress toward school academic goals	3.6	1.4	18
5. Distributes the results of student testing to teachers in a timely fashion	3.6	1.4	17
6. Informs teachers of the school's performance results on tests in written form (e.g., in memos or newsletters)	3.3	1.7	17
7. Informs students of the school's performance results	3.1	1.6	17
8. Identifies students whose performance on school tests indicates the need for special instruction or enrichment	2.9	1.8	15
9. Develops or finds the appropriate instructional program for students whose performance on tests indicates a need	2.9	1.7	15
OVERALL MEAN	3.3		

NOTES

1. The Chapter 1 coordinator is a curriculum specialist who could be called the vice principal.

2. In addition to the fact that overall Mr. Charles's scores are lower on the teacher questionnaire, the reader will note a large difference in his standard deviations as compared with the principals at Woodson and Foster schools. In fact, the standard deviations are usually twice as high for Mr. Charles and in some cases they are three times those of the other principals. This is due, it seems, in part, to the nature of Mr. Charles' personality. There was not an overall consensus among his staff about his leadership. Many teachers were very critical of his style while others were equally as adamant in their support for his style. The exploratory nature of this study prevents me from further speculating on the cause of this wide disparity in the standard deviation scores.

9

Analysis: Comparative Leadership

INTRODUCTION

In this chapter I compare the leadership of the African-American principals in my sample with the leadership of other principals as described in the research literature on principal leadership and academic achievement. I explore how relevant the general discussion of leadership is for African-American principals in more successful African-American elementary schools. This line of inquiry is necessary because some research suggests there may be differences in the way African-American principals lead. Also, I question the general applicability of principal leadership theory to African-American principals.

Next, I discuss, in some detail, the case of Collins Elementary School. While Collins is indeed a more successful school, its principal, Mr. Charles, operates in a very different way than do the other two principals, Mr. Brooks and Ms. Marshall. One explanation is that the principal does not matter at Collins. It is also possible that the situation at Collins is related to what researchers have described as substitutes for leadership (Kerr and Jermier, 1978).

FOSTER AND WOODSON ELEMENTARY SCHOOLS

Goal Development

Selznick and others stress the importance of leaders developing practical, realizable goals within institutions (Selznick, 1957). This characteristic appears consistently in descriptions of effective schools in the literature (Edmonds, 1979; Phi Delta Kappa, 1980).

At Woodson, school-level goals are developed by three groups—teachers and the principal, teachers, and students. Ms. Marshall is actively involved in developing goals. At Foster, Mr. Brooks's participation in meetings is the basis of his role as a guide in the goal development process.

On the teacher questionnaire, these two principals scored higher in this area than in the other three areas. This, again, is consistent with the relevant literature which shows goal development to be an important quality of leaders in effective organizations (Glenn, 1981; Selznick, 1957).

Energy Harnessing

This discussion relates to the ability of the principal, after setting the goals, to achieve some consensus among teachers about these priorities and to manage the school environment in such a way that teachers can do the work necessary to achieve these goals.

Principals harnessing the energy of teachers to work toward the collective goals is not directly addressed in the research on effective schools. This literature does, however, identify several significant components of energy harnessing. These qualities include being supportive of teachers (Gervals, 1982; Levine and Stark, 1981); providing a framework for collective decision making (New York State Office of Education, 1974; DeGuire, 1980); and emphasizing staff development aimed at teachers' weaknesses (Vallina, 1978).

Leadership theory also addresses the importance of energy harnessing. It emphasizes the need for leaders to encourage and develop the enthusiasm of the cohorts, and guide them in a collectively oriented direction (Burns, 1978; McGregor, 1966). Barnard emphasizes that the ability to convince people to actively support the organizational purposes is of paramount importance in cooperative systems. The establishment of goals, he says, is meaningless without selling the followers on the significance of the goals (Barnard, 1947).

Selznick (1957, p. 58) also emphasizes the need to encourage workers to support institutional goals:

Where implementation of policy depends to a considerable extent on attitudes and ways of thinking of personnel, an effort must be made to translate policy into an "organization doctrine" and to inculcate these ideas wherever necessary.... To mold the minds of individuals according to a definite pattern creates a homogeneous organization, and this is an enormous aid to communication. A broad context of "understood" meaning assures that in the performance of assigned tasks the spirit as well as the letter will be observed.

Selznick goes on to discuss the importance of leaders bringing the goals of internal interest groups (or the informal structure) and the goals of the organization into harmony with each other (Selznick, 1957).

In these two schools, the principals are able to keep the teachers working harmoniously and cooperatively. Some of Ms. Marshall's tactics include being a role model in and out of the classroom and scheduling one-on-one counseling sessions aimed at improving a particular teacher's skills.

At Foster, Mr. Brooks's careful selection of staff minimizes his difficulties in energy harnessing. In addition, he uses several techniques (such as classroom observation and staff meetings) to insure that teachers are in line with the school's goals. The ability of Ms. Marshall and Mr. Brooks to bring staff together is further enhanced by their support of teachers in the teachers' daily activities. For example, both principals told me that they prefer to keep the number of staff meetings to a minimum and that they try to minimize the amount of paper work that teachers are required to do.

I also observed, in these two principals, an awareness of some of the personal issues that were important to teachers. The teachers confirmed in the questionnaires that these principals are generally knowledgeable of staff personalities, problems, and interests. This support for teachers is consistent with Barnard's contention that, in addition to changing the attitudes of workers, leaders must also provide inducements or positive reinforcement. Barnard refers to these two techniques as the "method of persuasion" and the "method of incentives" (Barnard, 1947).

Communication Facilitation

Communication facilitation describes the effectiveness with which the principal communicates schoolwide goals and policies to the staff as well as his or her effectiveness in encouraging feedback from the staff on such matters.

If a principal talks regularly with teachers about issues such as teacher performance and curriculum, there is greater likelihood that the school will be successful (Wellisch et al., 1977; Jun, 1981). Such talks were certainly apparent at Woodson and Foster Elementary Schools. Ms. Marshall, for example, uses staff meetings, conferences with individual teachers, and student assemblies to discuss critical schoolwide issues.

Mr. Brooks used staff meetings and in-service programs to communicate the school's goals to his teachers. In large part, because of this, there is two-way communication at Foster.

Selznick (1957, p. 137) talks about the role which communication plays in organizations:

[Communications does] become vitally important when . . . given context [and] when . . . [it] serves the aim of fashioning a distinctive way of thinking or acting and thus helps establish the human foundation for achieving a particular set of goals.

Selznick, at another point, talks about the "social structure" through which communication must travel. Aspects of this structure are assigned roles, internal interest groups, social stratification, beliefs shared by staff, how deeply staff persons perceive their participation in the organization, and the dependency that occurs between different actors. The leader, Selznick says, must know how to deal with this structure in order to be effective. Mr. Brooks and Ms. Marshall have internalized an understanding of this structure in their schools, as evidenced by their many tactics encouraging two-way communication.

Instructional Management

For the purpose of this study, three areas are encompassed in instructional management: curriculum planning, teacher supervision, and the evaluation of student achievement.

Involvement by principals in the curriculum-planning process has been found to be important in bringing about school effectiveness (California State Department of Education, 1977; Weber, 1971). Also, principals in more successful schools are regularly involved in activities related to the supervision of teachers (Wellisch et al., 1977; Austin, 1979). Finally, research emphasizes the importance of the principal being involved in the evaluation of student achievement in order to increase schoool effectiveness (Edmonds, 1979; Felsenthal, 1982).

My exploratory observations of Ms. Marshall and Mr. Brooks did not support the conclusion of the Center for Educational Policy and Management (1982) that principals do not spend substantial time in instructional activities. Ms. Marshall is actively involved in the instructional management areas of curriculum planning, evaluation of student achievement, and teacher supervision. Mr. Brooks is also involved in all curriculum planning at Foster. In addition, he is regularly active in the evaluation of student achievement and in staff supervision matters. His consultant/guide role in these instructional areas helps facilitate the smooth flow of work and the warm familylike atmosphere that permeates the school.

COLLINS ELEMENTARY SCHOOL

Introduction

There are some differences in the leadership of Mr. Charles when compared to the leadership of the other two principals. These differences are based, in part, on Mr. Charles' tendency to delegate authority.

Mr. Charles delegates the authority for leadership in the development of goals. Also, the coordinator, and not Mr. Charles, appears to be the pivotal figure in the harnessing of the staff's energy. She oversees in-service programs and staff meetings.

Though he delegates much of his authority, Mr. Charles does communicate the school's goals. He emphasizes these goals in assemblies, staff meetings, and usually as a follow-up to discipline problems in meetings with students.

In the areas of curriculum planning, the evaluation of student achievement, and teacher supervision, Mr. Charles' strategy, again, is to delegate the authority to the coordinator and resource teachers. Mr. Charles pointed out to me that a principal in an effective school needs a good management team. He does have one and the quality of these people contributes to his ability to have a more successful school while delegating much of his authority.

Mr. Charles is not directly involved in leadership in the four areas that I explored. While one of my initial assumptions was that the principal is a key factor in more successful African-American elementary schools, the situation at Collins suggests that, at this school, this may not be necessarily true. That is, it is possible that Collins may be more successful without leadership being provided by Mr. Charles. The causes of success could be other variables. One of the teachers at Collins supported this speculation when she said, in regard to the reasons for the success at Collins, "I'm not sure it's the principal here."

Substitutes for Leadership Theory

There is a school of thought which suggests that school leadership can be provided by anyone (e.g., specialists, assistant principals, department heads, etc.) and that, therefore, the principal is less important than the current research on instructional leadership would suggest (Kerr and Jermier, 1978; Gersten, Carnine, and Green, 1982; Center for Educational Policy and Management, 1982; Manasse, 1985). In discussing the limited research addressing this concept, Manasse (1985, p. 448) describes these substitutes as follows:

Substitutes for leadership include any characteristics of subordinates, task or organization that ensure subordinates will clearly understand their roles, know how to do the work, be highly motivated, and be satisfied with the job.

This description provides another possible explanation for the situation at Collins. A number of studies have highlighted situations where instructional programs were successful in the absence of principals serving as instructional managers (Good and Grouws, 1979; Kennedy, 1978).

Mr. Charles does delegate much of his administrative authority. He is not directly involved in the formulation of school goals; his is not the major role in harnessing the energy of the staff; the coordinator and the resource teachers are mostly responsible for communication between the administration and the faculty, and also have primary responsibility for the three instructional management areas: curriculum, evaluation of student achievement, and teacher supervision. In discussing his role as principal at Collins, Mr. Charles told me:

I have had some good people assisting me. I've had some good coordinators that I have selected. I've got a good one now. I had one that just made assistant principal. So it hasn't—one of the things as you probably can guess is that to be fairly effective in getting the school moving forward, you can't do it yourself. You've got to get some other people. So what I do is I've had the resource people and the coordinators to work.

They get out and they pitch in and they work. And I think I've got a good—you'll meet these people. I think you'll be able to see we've got some good people in leadership. We've got some good people in the management team. And that's what's so important.

This wide-scale delegation of authority, while very different from the leadership style of the other principals, does not necessarily suggest that Mr. Charles is not a leader. Researchers who articulate this substitute for leadership theory, like others, acknowledge the fact that a leader's utility is in seeing that the various leadership functions are fulfilled (Center for Educational Policy and Management, 1982; Lipham, 1981; Morris, 1981; Barnard, 1947). If this is so, this delegation of authority is merely reflective of a shared leadership model, a legitimate variation on traditional principal leadership (Duckworth, 1981).

One researcher has described what appears to be two dominant principal leadership styles (Manasse 1985, p. 453):

those who personally have an understanding of, and goals for, their organizations . . . [and] . . . those who understand organizational processes well enough to provide support to other visionaries in their schools.

While clear delineations are difficult (due to the nature of these descriptions and due to the exploratory nature of this study), it appears that Mr. Brooks and Ms. Marshall fit somewhat into the first group. Mr. Charles' approach is more difficult to classify. The data suggest several possibilities. It is possible that he is utilizing substitutes for leadership which would put him in the second category of dominant leadership styles. On the other hand, there is substantial reason to speculate that his leadership is unimportant in the success of the school and that he does not fit into either category. Another possibility is that Mr. Charles is not providing leadership at all at Collins. The two latter cases would suggest that the success at Collins is due to the work of teachers or some other factor or set of factors. Further clarification on the exact nature of Mr. Charles' leadership is not possible given the exploratory nature of this study.

SUMMARY

At Foster and Woodson Elementary Schools staff unity is based on internalizing both goals and the values inherent in those goals. It seems to permeate the staff, affecting decisions and attitudes on many levels. This widespread internalization of the school's goals is what Selznick calls institutional integrity. The major function of leaders, according to him, is to build this integrity, something that the principals in both of these schools seem to have done.

Yet there is no formula for leadership in more effective schools. Mr. Charles leads very differently than the other principals. He is not directly involved in the four leadership areas under study, though he has been able to see that others in his school have performed. The data, in fact, do not allow determination of the importance of his leadership.

REFERENCES

Austin, G. R. 1979. "Exemplary schools and the search for effectiveness." *Educational Leadership* 37, no. 1: 10–14.

Barnard, C. I. 1947. *The Functions of the Executive*. Cambridge, Mass.: Harvard University Press.

Burns, J. M. 1978. *Leadership*. New York: Harper and Row.

California State Department of Education. 1977. *1977 California School Effectiveness Study: The First Year: 1974–75*. Sacramento, Calif.: Office of Program Evaluation and Research.

Center for Educational Policy and Management. 1982. "The principal's role: How do we reconcile expectations with reality?" *R&D Perspectives*. Eugene: University of Oregon, 1–8.

DeGuire, M. R. 1980. "The role of the elementary principal in influencing reading achievement." Ph.D. diss., University of Colorado.

Duckworth, K. 1981. *Linking Educational Policy and Management with Student Achievement*. Center for Educational Policy and Management, University of Oregon.

Edmonds, R. 1979. "Effective schools for the urban poor." *Educational Leadership* 37, no. 1: 15–24.

Felsenthal, H. 1982. "Factors influencing school effectiveness: An ecological analysis of an effective school." Paper presented at the Annual Meeting of the American Educational Research Association, New York.

Gersten, R., D. Carnine, and S. Green. 1982. "The principal as instructional leader: A second look." *Educational Leadership* 40, no. 1: 47–50.

Gervais, R. L. 1982. "How do principals affect reading achievement?" *PTA Today* 7: 25.

Glenn, B. C. 1981. "What works? An examination of effective schools for poor black children." Cambridge, Mass.: Center for Law and Education, Harvard University.

Good, T., and D. Grouws. 1979. "The Missouri mathematics effectiveness project." *Journal of Educational Psychology* 71, no. 3: 355–62.

Jun, S. 1981. "Principal leadership, teacher job satisfaction and student achievement in selected Korean elementary schools." Ph.D. diss., Florida State University.

Kennedy, M. 1978. "Findings from the follow through planned variation study." *Educational Researcher* 7, no. 6: 3–11.

Kerr, S., and J. Jermier. "Substitutes for leadership: Their meaning and measurement." *Organizational Behavior and Human Performance* 22, no. 3: 375–403.

Levine, D. U., and J. Stark. 1981. "Extended summary and conclusion: Instructional and organizational arrangements and processes for improving academic achievement at inner city elementary schools." Kansas City, Mo.: University of Missouri, Kansas City, School of Education, Center for the Study of Metropolitan Problems in Education.

Lipham, J. M. 1981. *Effective Principal, Effective School*. Reston, Va.: National Association of Secondary School Principals.

Manasse, A. L. 1985. "Improving conditions for principal effectiveness: Policy implications of research." *Elementary School Journal* 85, no. 3: 439–63.

McGregor, D. 1966. *Leadership and Motivation*. Cambridge, Mass.: MIT.

Morris, V. C., et al. 1981. *Discretionary Decision-Making in a Large Education Organization: A Report of a Research Project Funded* by the National Institute of Education. Chicago: College of Education, University of Illinois at Chicago Circle.

New York State Office of Education. 1974. "School factors influencing reading achievement: A case study of two inner city schools." Albany, N.Y.: Office of Education Performance Review.

Phi Delta Kappa. 1980. *Why Do Some Urban Schools Succeed? The Phi Delta Kappan Study of Exceptional Urban Elementary Schools.* Bloomington, Ind.: Phi Delta Kappa.

Selznick, P. 1957. *Leadership in Administration: A Sociological Interpretation.* Evanston, Ill.: Row, Peterson.

Vallina, S. A. 1978. "Analysis of observed critical task performance of Title I ESEA principals, state of Illinois." Ed.D. diss., Loyola University.

Weber, G. 1971. *Inner City Children Can Be Taught To Read: Four Successful Schools.* Washington, D.C.: Council for Basic Education.

Wellisch, J. B., et al. 1978. "School management and organization in successful schools. *Sociology of Education* 51, no. 3: 211–26.

10

Other Leadership Qualities of African-American Principals

INTRODUCTION

Perhaps the most meaningful finding in this study is that there appear to be three qualities that these principals all hold in common. Each principal appears to demonstrate a commitment to the education of African-American children, a compassion for, and understanding of, their students and of the communities in which they work, and a confidence in the ability of all African-American children to learn.[1]

The fact that these qualities appear to be shared by all of the principals is important because it raises the question of the significance, for African-American principals, of these three characteristics in relation to the four qualities that I sought to explore. It is possible that, given the unique characteristics of these African-American schools (e.g., economic, academic, cultural, and social), these three qualities supersede all others in importance in bringing about success.

QUALITIES SHARED BY PRINCIPALS

Commitment to the Education of African-American Children

Mr. Charles. Mr. Brooks, and Ms. Marshall all appear to have as their first priority the education of the children in their schools. Some other principals, in Ms. Marshall's view, have other priorities—money high among them.

The commitment of these principals to the education of African-American children became evident in discussions, interviews, and direct observation of their activities. It was typified in the following comment by Mr. Brooks: "I've had chances to move to the North [white] end of town, but I don't know, it's the feeling I think I have for the black community."

One experienced teacher at Foster said of Mr. Brooks:

I've never seen a principal who is with the kids as much as he is. He's on yard duty all the time. He's at breakfast. He talks to them. He really does talk to them. He knows their names. He keeps track of them. I have a kid that's a behavior problem. He [Mr. Brooks] noticed that . . . [Ronald] hadn't been in trouble for three days. He really is observant. He picks up the details so you know he must care, because he picks them up and they're little, they're minor and they're something you'd think only a teacher would know. That's what I see and I think that goes back to the fact that his first priority is the kids.

This teacher went on to say:

I know that the child is really important [to him]. Mr. [Brooks] has spoken to us more than once on how to make our childen feel good about themselves and [about the fact that] they have rights and that we are to treat them as we want to be treated. [In addition, he stresses that] bad conduct will not be tolerated. Also, self-value is very, very important here and is stressed along with responsibility.

I've been stifled in other areas because my administrator's priorities were not with the kids and that's frustrating. And that's why I'm feeling really at home here because this is a unique school. Everything that Mr. [Brooks] does, I really believe, is in the kids' best interest. And you can really tell because he goes to his teachers and finds out. He's just squared away in that area. It's what's best for the kids and then everything else is secondary.

The first week of school, I had forty-three kids and I just thought that was terrible for me. And he said, no, it's not for you I'm worried. It's the kids. He goes, you can't feel sorry for yourself. You gotta feel sorry for the kids. And it's true. It was bad on me, but it was worse for them. He just really has it together in that area, as far as I can see.

Another teacher at Foster concurred: "He genuinely cares—probably more than any other man I've ever met—for the kids and their well-being and that's what makes it click. When you get people who share his concern with him, it all meshes."

Indeed, Mr. Brooks's classroom observations were not for show. It was clear from the teacher interviews and teacher questionnaires that classroom observation is part of his daily routine. Also, he seemed to be genuinely concerned with the progress of the students. He would look at the desk work of several students and challenge them to explain it.

During one of our talks, Mr. Charles said, "we must challenge the children continuously." In discussing the uniqueness of the African-American child, he added, "[the] black child has all of the white child's problems and his [own] and I'm not gonna add a persecution problem to that." In most, if not all, of the discipline-related discussions which Mr. Charles had with students (or with students and parents) his focus was invariably on the importance of academics, for the particular child and the classroom disruption caused by the misbehavior. Regardless of the problem, he always seemed to express the importance of the student's academic success. Also, in his various discussions with teachers, Mr. Charles was always emphasizing the need for them to push the children intellectually. He seemed to feel that some of the teachers did not have the confidence in the potential of some of their students.

I talked with Ms. Marshall about maintaining her commitment to African-American children and the commitment of her teachers (in the face of such a high level of student transiency) and she said:

It goes back to the kind of teachers I have here. The kind of values I have articulated. We're not here just for a job. With the one child that you think you may not be helping to develop academically you might be sparking something that later in life might change his whole academic outlook. So it's not how low or how often you're getting a change. It's doing and giving your best and your all that year 'cause that'll be the only chance you'll get and somehow that's worked.

When talking with me about what she described as the misplaced priorities of some principals, Ms. Marshall said, "Principals should ask, why am I here? It's not to hire people, but to serve children." Indeed, her relationship with her students and their families, on one level, takes precedence over her responsibilities to the central office. One day during my observations, Ms. Marshall was scheduled to leave for a principal meeting at slightly after one o'clock. She chose instead to meet with a parent, who had unexpectedly come in, before leaving. After she met with that parent she met with another parent who had come in and insisted on seeing her. Before leaving for the meeting, for which she was now close to one hour late, she explained to me that the situation at the school site was her key responsibility and that, as a result, she had no misgivings about being late for the principal meeting.

Compassion for, and Understanding of, African-American Children and their Communities

In discussing African-American principals in African-American schools, Mr. Brooks told me:

Being black is not enough. One needs to be sensitive to the needs of black students and to the total black community. I think they ought to be not only sensitive, but knowledgeable about the needs of black children.

In expounding on those needs, Mr. Brooks added:

I won't say that they're any different than the needs of white children, but I think there is a degree of being more sensitive, in that I feel that where we have more broken homes, more one-parent homes and, in many instances, more low-income families and more people on AFDC, I think it calls for a kind of a person who would be knowledgeable and caring for those kinds of, not disabilities, but those kinds of things that are well . . . much of it is in our black community.

Here we have support for the significance of a class culture. Mr. Brooks suggests that a key factor in relating to African-American children understanding is their socioeconomic status.

Mr. Brooks seems to personify his blueprint for principals. He appears to know all of his students' brothers, sisters, parents, and grandparents (as well as most of the people who pass by the school in the afternoon). He seems to continually run into former students. When discussing the important factors that set Foster apart from other schools in its district, one teacher said of Mr. Brooks: "[He] knows [the] community. He's lived in this area for a long time and the sensitivity makes a big difference, I feel."

In discussing Mr. Brooks's personal relationshiip with his students, another teacher at Foster said:

Some principals will not put their arms around the kids because, you know, this threat of child abuse—you better not touch 'em. Now Mr. [Brooks] will touch the kids. Some of them [principals] keep that distance. You over there and me over here, and don't bother me. I've kinda noticed that. There's like more of a closeness with this one [Mr. Brooks].

Mr. Charles' actions regarding discipline demonstrated his compassion and understanding. He is aware of the fact that disciplinary measures must not only fit the offense, but that they must also fit the student. On more than one occasion, Mr. Charles discussed with me appropriate and inappropriate discipline for specific children. John, a student who seemed to get into trouble often, was in Mr. Charles' office one day because he had not gotten on the bus after school on the previous day. He had gone to a friend's house. After dealing with the situation and excusing John, Mr. Charles explained to me that suspensions were not an effective way of dealing with John.

The situation in the assembly with the students who were placed in the corner also demonstrates not only Mr. Charles' emphasis on consistent discipline but his understanding of the need for appropriate disciplinary measures. On another occasion, after talking with two students regarding their misbehavior, Mr. Charles made arrangements for them to come to school early on the next day to clean up the front yard. In a final instance, a student and teacher came into Mr. Charles' office regarding a discipline problem. The student had been repeatedly laughing and talking out loud in the classroom. After a brief discussion, the principal had arrived at a diagnosis of the problem and excused the student from the room. He went on to suggest to the teacher that the student was lacking adequate academic stimulation, and he encouraged her to provide additional work for the child.

In discussing the failure of educators to reason with African-American students, Mr. Charles said:

You can do anything, demand anything from the kid. Be as firm and strong as you want. But what we don't do with the black kids is we don't tell them why. We don't reason with them.

A teacher at Woodson best described Ms. Marshall's compassion and understanding when talking about the way in which children at Woodson relate to their principal:

They can relate to a black principal because the principal is a mother or father figure. . . . I think when she [Ms. Marshall] speaks . . . they're used to that authoritative woman at home too. [Marie] [Marshall] has that softness . . . where the kids are free to come up to her and hug her and, yet in still, they know she might paddle their butts the next day. So I think there's a nice balance between the kids and [Marie] where they'll work hard when she asks them to. They know they're gonna get some type of reward or they're gonna get praised or they know they're gonna be scolded or they're gonna be paddled—some of them. I think they've got that love 'cause she's like a mama. You know they're gonna get it.

In school you're here to learn and plus she's a good role
model. . . . They feel free to run up and touch her. A lot of times
teachers don't want you to touch them. It's a nice feeling where they
feel close to her and they try to achieve.

Ms. Marshall shared with the other principals a unique
understanding of the need to be tuned into the heartbeat of the
community in which she worked. She told me that "the par-
ticularities of the culture of a community are of utmost importance for principals. A principal cannot rely simply on the
norms of the society in general." She further explained her
point, using assertive discipline as an example:

I cannot see assertive discipline in its so-called true form for the kids in
inner cities. There aren't homes that provide organized manners. So
when you state your rules you almost have to use an eclectic form,
because you just don't have kids coming from the kinds of homes
that—once you set up your rules, three strikes, you're out, and I mean
they're out in like three minutes, because they're gonna do a number of
things to just make your plan totally unworkable. So it's like going into
a classroom, teaching etiquette. First teaching standards before you
can even get to a discipline plan. So that's the job of the principal.
Many of the teachers come in thinking they can try that, and it's failed
and they have been totally crushed. So I have to stop and say many of
the children who are from the inner city areas, who have not had the
kinds of backgrounds and home structure that this program would
lend itself to. You have to go back and look at the program itself and
take the best parts that you feel are workable.

She added that "you can't look for two- and three-year gains. A
lot of the children we're getting that are low are not low
because they cannot attain or attend the information." She explained that many of these students, coming to Woodson for the
first time, have either had a lot of substitute teachers or have
had poor teachers and were never taught the prerequisite skills
or they were from highly transient families and had been moved
from school to school several times.

Ms. Marshall went on to describe the "poor background" of
the students at Woodson:

When I say poor background, it's generally an unorganized home background. Mother going one way, whether it's going to work or family going one way. The family structure isn't very close. There's no father in the home. So, it looks as if, as I look at it, the black principal has to be the one almost looking and playing God sometimes, in terms of looking at values, looking at past history. . . . No matter what new innovations or methods are coming in in education you have to look at the needs of your children, the cultural background of your children. . . . You have to go back and look at how we, as a people, functioned. The extended family that was once very important died out and I'm finding at a school like this we have a gang problem because we don't have extended families. We have problems of child care with kindergarteners going home at noon, or we have, for example, kindergarteners whose mothers have to work and they set a clock 'cause the kid can't tell when to go to school. The mother dresses the five-year-old. She sets the clock. When the clock rings you push a little button and then you leave to go to school. That shouldn't be. With extended families, we didn't have that kind of problem. You didn't have children just walking the streets alone. You had brothers, sisters, uncles, [and] cousins, who helped with school work and whatever. Now you have a totally different problem existing because we are saying that was something that was no good or whatever we say. So I think you first have to look at culture. That's most important. You have to look at what functions for the culture.

She added:

In this school environment parents believe in corporal punishment, but I had new teachers who don't come from this culture [and] who did not believe in corporal punishment. No one uses corporal punishment here but me, when it's used. You have to look at those values that the people hold dear and build on those. You can't just look at what society's asking as a whole and say I'm gonna run my school according to what is happening now. A good example being individualization of instruction, the learning center approach and all the kinds of things that came out several years ago. That would not work in a black school because the children could not handle the freedom of scheduling and whatever. You'd have to start with a very structured background with the youngsters and then build into teaching children how to schedule because that was just too much. So you have to look at, again, the culture, the values, those kinds of objectives you want articulated for your children. And then you have to be the one to see that they're implemented, whether it be monitoring those teachers [or] selecting those teachers.

Seemingly, it is their compassion and understanding which enables these principals to effectively choose teachers. In discussing the selection of teachers, Ms. Marshall said to me:

Selecting teachers in this kind of an environment is key. If you've got a teacher who is opposed to structure in the classroom, who does things haphazardly, [and] who doesn't plan, that teacher's gonna be less capable of doing anything in an environment like this.

Whenever possible, Ms. Marshall hires new teachers as substitutes, for a week or so, so that she can observe them in the classroom and talk with them before committing the district to a long-term contract. This is what was occurring with the three new teachers when I first visited Woodson in the fall; only two of them survived. One of Ms. Marshall's teachers said in an interview, "She scrutinizes when she hires. Very rarely do they slip through the cracks."

Mr. Charles at Collins also knows of the need to have teachers who are aware of the uniqueness of the African-American student. On several occasions when talking informally with me, he discussed fears of losing such conscientious teachers and the need to get more teachers with the required sensitivities.

Mr. Brooks described "good teachers" as follows:

I think the classroom teacher to me is the key. The leadership that the principal shows toward having the teacher to go toward the goals and objectives, I think is very paramount. But if you get good teachers, the principal's role is relatively easy. By good teachers, I mean those teachers who are very sensitive to the needs of, let's say, our black children, who do more than just come to school and teach and go home. Teachers who show a definite interest in the total black community—the home, the lifestyles, and all those things that enter into what I feel is a very well-rounded knowledge of the children that you're working with.

Confidence in the Educability of African-American Children

The principals I observed appear to be committed to equity for African-American students. They seem confident that they can provide all African-American children with a better education.

Though Mr. Brooks did not say very much to me in regard to his confidence in the ability of African-American students to perform well, his interactions with teachers and students demonstrated this confidence. During classroom observations, he constantly challenged students regarding the work they had done and he was always supportive in terms of inspiring them to do even better work and to not settle for mediocrity.

On several occasions, I overheard Mr. Brooks encouraging teachers who had become somewhat despondent over the academic performance of students. He would remind them that just by trying a little harder, they would be able to contribute to the children's increased learning. His confidence was reflected in his answer to a question I asked regarding the way in which teachers deal with students who have academic deficiencies:

I don't feel that there is enough zeroing in on the deficiencies. I think our program should be revised in order to really zero in on these particular areas where a student is most weak. I don't think enough of that is being done. Not only in this school, [but] districtwide.

The suggestion here is that, again, with just a little more pushing, additional academic success could be attained.

In speaking about this confidence, Mr. Charles told me:

I think we're doing an excellent job, but that doesn't mean that we're pleased. Because actually, our goal would be to have something like 70 to 75 percent of the children achieving on the Comprehensive Test of Basic Skills (CTBS) and I think that is attainable. . . . But the point is that I believe that this can be attained with the present staff, with the present community, [and] with the present children.

The basic philosophy we try to have here with the staff and with the leadership is that we're not content or satisfied with our success. If one child is not achieving at his maximum potential, or close to that maximum potential, then we've failed.

He went on to say:

I'm aware of the bell curve, and I understand all of that, but on the other hand, I'm sure you know, and I know, that there are schools in certain areas like Chicago and New York that are private and some very unorthodox private schools that are religious. They take people right off the street and they have remarkable achievement levels. I know they have controls that we don't have, but nevertheless, I think that we can use some of their techniques and some of their motivation and approximate some of their results.

At another point, Mr. Charles reminded me that "the black child is extremely intelligent, creative, perceptive, imaginative, and responsive to difficult tasks." He went on to say that "what we're saying is that the [black] child can respond to what we call the crisis skills—the skills that are at risk." All three principals, echoing Mr. Charles, believe that all African-American children can learn regardless of their background.

Mr. Charles told me, on several occasions, that he felt that some teachers were unnecessarily holding children back academically. I heard him encouraging teachers more than once to challenge the children with additional work. In one case, a parent came in who was concerned because her perception was that her daughter, Shawn, had not been sufficiently challenged academically. After a lengthy discussion with the parent, the school psychologist, and the teacher, and a review of the child's permanent record, it appeared as though Mr. Charles agreed with the parent (he later told me that he did and that he was not confident that the teacher was likely to begin to challenge Shawn). Mr. Charles then called in the mentor teacher and attempted to make her feel that she was involved in the decision—which he then made—to put Shawn in her class, thereby improving the chances of progress.[2]

Ms. Marshall's confidence in the ability of her African-American students to learn is evident in her consistent desire to analyze test scores and to see that any necessary remediation for students is done. She does not appear to think in terms of a lack of ability on the part of students. Instead, she is constantly encouraging teachers to conduct diagnoses and follow through for students. She told me that she expects teachers to efficiently and quickly diagnose and prescribe work for students. She focuses many of the staff in-service programs on these instructional skills.

In one instance, I observed a teacher come into Ms. Marshall's office three times during the day to ask about having a new student placed in a lower grade. The student, it seems, had scored poorly on placement tests. The teacher felt that the student would not be able to perform well in her class. Ms. Marshall was very hesitant to agree to moving the child. She wanted to be sure that every effort was made to accurately assess the child's proficiencies before he was moved to a lower grade.

Even in the instance when a teacher came in to seek help with a new student who was 87 percent deaf in one ear, Ms. Marshall was genuinely concerned about what services could be offered at Woodson so that the child could learn at his maximum potential.

SUMMARY

Ms. Marshall and Mr. Brooks appear to provide direct leadership in the four areas examined in this study. Mr. Charles does not. Still, all of the principals in my sample seem to have something in common. There is substantial evidence that they each have commitment to the education of African-American children, compassion for, and understanding of, their students and of the communities in which they work, and confidence in the ability of all African-American children to learn. The exploratory nature of this study prevents further speculation as to the relative importance of these qualities and the other four qualities. However, these three qualities do appear to be worthy of further consideration in subsequent research.

NOTES

1. Mr. Charles, at Collins, operates his school differently than the other two principals in the study. He delegates much of his responsibility in the four leadership areas examined in this study. In spite of the contrast between Mr. Charles and the other two principals, the results of my observations suggest that all of the principals in my sample, including Mr. Charles, do have these qualities in common which appear to contribute to the success of their schools.

2. The Accra Unified School District has mentor teachers at each school. These are seasoned teachers with reputations for excellence in teaching. The mentor teacher at Collins, Ms. Jefferson, whom I observed on several occasions in her classroom, lived up to this reputation.

11

Summary and Implications

INTRODUCTION

School principals are essential to school success (Sarasan, 1971). They are responsible for all functions that take place in and around the school. Their leadership sets the ambiance of the school, the atmosphere for learning, the level of professionalism and morale of teachers, and the degree of concern for what students may or may not become. Principals are the main link between the school and the community. The way principals perform in that capacity largely determines the attitude of teachers, students, and parents about the school and consequently affects school success.

In this chapter I offer a brief summary of my findings focusing first on the framework, set out earlier, and second on the three research questions posed. I then offer some conclusions. Next I present a brief discussion on some implications, emphasizing the areas of theory and research. Finally, I discuss several suggestions for future research.

BRIEF REVIEW OF RESULTS/FINDINGS

I employed a framework based upon the contention in the literature that the leadership of the principal affects the behavior of the teachers which subsequently affects the achievement of students (see figure 2.1.) While I did not look at these two relationships, I did focus on the impact that the leadership of the principal has on aspects of the school environment. The selection of this focus was based on the belief that this relationship affects relationships with teachers and, indirectly, relationships with students.

There were indications from teacher interviews that at Foster, Mr. Brooks is often able to bring staff together to focus on specific tasks. Teachers at Foster are generally receptive to his requests. His individual principal/teacher conferences with teachers, according to them, are very effective in affecting their behavior. These data present a picture of the impact which Mr. Brooks has on selected aspects of the school environment. If, in fact, a principal is able to effectively harness the energy of staff, there is good reason to believe that he or she can then steer teacher behavior toward the collective goals of the school.

At Woodson, teachers agreed that Ms. Marshall is almost always effective in affecting the behavior of teachers. It is, in part, Ms. Marshall's fairness in dealing with teachers that enables her to get teacher to cooperate, according to one teacher. Here again, the principal's effectiveness in bringing staff together to work collectively suggests a greater likelihood that staff will perform in the best interest of the school.

Generally, these two principals have provided assertive leadership, creating a school climate that is conducive to encouraging teachers to exhibit appropriate behavior for the improvement of academic achievement. That is, by providing direct leadership in goal development, energy harnessing, communication facilitation, and instructional management, these leaders have moved their schools one step closer to what Selznick calls institutionalization. In institutionalization, a work environment exists where the staff work together so well that their attitudes, behaviors, and decisions are influenced by the collective atmosphere. The data suggest that this is happening at these two schools.

Though Mr. Charles does not play a direct leadership role at Collins in the area of energy harnessing, he does make sure that his management team affects the behavior of teachers. In doing so, he affects the climate of the school in an important way. That is, his different style of leadership—emphasizing delegation—still appears to have an impact on the school climate and on, I suggest, teacher behavior and student academic achievement.

I addressed three research questions in this book:

1. How do African-American principals in more successful African-American elementary schools demonstrate goal development, energy harnessing, communication facilitation, and instructional management (i.e., a regular involvement in (a) the evaluation of academic achievement, (b) curriculum planning, and (c) teacher supervision) in their schools?

2. How does the leadership of African-American principals in more successful African-American elementary schools compare with the leadership of other principals as described in the research literature?

3. What other leadership qualities, if any, do African-American principals in more successful African-American elementary schools hold in common with each other?

Question 1

Mr. Brooks at Foster and Ms. Marshall at Woodson appear to be directly involved in providing leadership in each of the areas addressed in this study. Both principals are directly involved in the development of goals at their school. They encourage teachers to work together through activities such as providing curriculum materials, teaming teachers, and having formal and informal discussions with teachers. Mr. Brooks and Ms. Marshall stress school policies and goals with teachers in staff meetings and in-service programs. Finally, they guide their staffs in the area of instructional management. They keep abreast of the curriculum in their schools, they observe classroom lessons, and they monitor schoolwide testing and provide feedback to teachers.

The situation at Collins is somewhat different. In each of these areas, Mr. Charles delegates much of his authority to his coordinator and resource teachers. Mr. Charles plays a minor role in the development of goals at Collins. He is often ineffective in his attempts to draw staff together. He is also, according to teachers, frequently offensive when attempting to communicate goals and school policies to staff. As an instructional leader, Mr. Charles is not directly involved. He leaves most of the leadership in curriculum planning, teacher supervision, and achievement evaluation to his coordinator and resource teachers.

Question 2

Mr. Brooks and Ms. Marshall both emphasize goal development in their schools much in the same way as described in the literature. The leadership of these principals also mirrors the research findings in the areas of energy harnessing, communication facilitation, and instructional management.

Mr. Charles is only minimally involved in goal development at his school and is not responsible for harnessing the energy of his teachers. While the literature suggests that these principals would be directly involved in the development of easily translatable school goals, Mr. Charles is not. He also does not take an active role in rallying teachers around school goals. He is irregularly involved in communication facilitation, and is not directly involved in instructional management in his school. Though he does attempt to communicate school goals to teachers, Mr. Charles is often ineffective and rarely solicits feedback from teachers. As an instructional manager, Mr. Charles' indirect leadership is inconsistent with the direct involvement implicit in the findings of the previous literature on principal leadership. His leadership doe not compare favorably with that which is described in the literature on principals in more successful schools.

Question 3

There are two findings of interest. First, there is more than one leadership style which principals exhibit in African-American

elementary schools. One is the forceful, assertive leader. Brief-
ly, the forceful, assertive leaders are those who are called, in
much of the effective schools literature, the "strong leaders."
They are intimately involved in all areas of the school's operation, and specifically in the instructional program. Seldom do
they delegate authority to others in the school. They are directly
involved throughout the day in activities geared toward improving the level of academic success of the school. In my sample, Mr. Brooks and Ms. Marshall fit this category.

Mr. Charles does not fall into this category. He delegates
much of his authority and is only minimally involved in instructional matters. It is however, difficult to characterize his leadership style based on the data from this exploratory study. In fact,
the relatively high standard deviations on the teacher questionnaires suggest that there is no consensus among the staff at Collins regarding the nature of Mr. Charles' leadership. Several
possibilities exist. It is possible that his leadership successfully
centers around his careful selection of administrative staff to
whom he delegates much of his authority. It is also possible that
students score relatively high on academic achievement tests
because of factors that do not include the leadership of Mr.
Charles. That is, Mr. Charles' behavior may not constitute
leadership at all or his leadership may be so occasional that it is
insignificant. While I began with the assumption that principal
leadership matters, it is possible, given the data from Collins,
that, at this school, this is not the case.

The second finding is that regardless of which leadership approach is employed, there are some qualities that the three
African-American principals hold in common. Specifically, it
appears that these principals share a commitment to the education of African-American children, compassion for, and
understanding of, their students and their communities, and a
confidence in the ability of all African-American children to
learn.

The importance of this finding lies in the fact that, unlike the
four qualities which I began exploring, these qualities were
held by all three of the principals. This suggests the need to

explore their relative importance for African-American principals in African-American elementary schools.

CONCLUSIONS

There appear to be four major conclusions derived from the findings of this study:

1. There appears to be more than one leadership style exhibited by African-American principals in more successful African-American elementary schools.

2. Some African-American principals in more successful African-American elementary schools provide direct leadership in areas of goal development, energy harnessing, communication facilitation, and instructional management in a way which is similar to other principals as described in the literature.

3. Some African-American principals in more successful African-American elementary schools do not provide direct leadership in the areas of goal development, energy harnessing, communication facilitation, and instructional management.

4. It appears that African-American principals in more successful African-American elementary schools hold three qualities in common with each other:

   a. a strong commitment to the education of African-American children

   b. a deep compassion for, and understanding of, their students and of the communities in which they work

   c. a sincere confidence in the ability of all African-American children to learn

Perhaps the most important finding is the last one, as it suggests that these three qualities may be more important than the four which I set out to examine. Unlike the original four qualities, these three were found in all of the principals. This conclusion is not surprising as aspects of it are supported in the literature. For example researchers have suggested that effective communication and interaction come about when two people share a culture (MacLennan, 1975; Kochman, 1981). Shared culture enables principals to better understand their students and their communities. In the final analysis, this understanding could positively affect academic achievement.

Similarly, researchers have suggested that a belief in the educability of one's students by a principal has an indirect impact on the academic achievement of students (Edmonds, 1979; Wellisch et al., 1978). It also follows that these principals would hold high expectations for their students because other researchers have shown that where educators have low expectations for student performance, the students invariably perform poorly (Rist, 1970; Beady and Hansell, 1981).

IMPLICATIONS OF FINDINGS

Implications for Research on Theory and Practice

There has been minimal testing (or even citing) of the works of Barnard and Selznick elsewhere (Peters and Waterman, 1983). This gap is particularly relevant in the effective schools' research on principals. In this book I have, to some small degree, expanded the operational implications of their works. There is an indication from my findings that Barnard's key roles for leaders, and Selznick's discussion of the development of institutional integrity, are directly applicable to schools. There were clear indications that, in two of the three schools, the principals exhibited Barnard's role for leaders—defining goals, harnessing the energy of staff and facilitating two-way communication. Also, in these two schools, there was an institutional climate that seemed to affect the behavior, attitudes, and decisions of teachers. Two of the three principals emphasize goal development, energy harnessing, and communication facilitation. In addition, these principals, in their leadership, do embody Selznick's notion of striving for institutional integrity.

While this was not a theory-testing study, I do offer some suggestions as to how the works of Barnard, Selznick, and others

in organizational theory may be applicable in the public sec-
tor—specifically in elementary school administration.

Also of importance is a need for the further development of
conceptual and methodological tools to forge the connection
between the data on principal leadership and academic
achievement (Manasse, 1985). Practitioners and researchers
alike have known for decades that there is a link between what
a principal does in his or her school and student scores on
schoolwide achievement tests. The exact nature of this link—its
strength and the specific aspects of principal leadership that affect academic achievement—have yet to be determined. There
has been inadequate theoretical development linking these two
phenomena. These theories must be developed and tested in
order for us to better understand the complex linkages.

For example, I did not find support for the frequent claim in
the principal leadership literature that principals, and African-
American principals in particular, in more successful schools
tend to be actively involved in the larger community surrounding their schools (Morris et al., 1981; Monteiro, 1977). While this
was definitely the case with Mr. Brooks at Foster, Ms. Marshall
appeared considerably less involved in the community and Mr.
Charles appeared only marginally involved, if at all. Theoretical
linkages between the principal's community involvement and
students' academic achievement were unsupported.

Exploratory studies like this one are important initial steps.
As studies suggest areas of principal leadership that affect the
school environment, researchers can utilize this information to
further develop and test theories to confirm or disconfirm the
limited existing evidence and provide new evidence. With
studies such as this one, researchers may be inspired to construct related theory-testing studies to give practitioners and
researchers a better understanding of this link.

SUGGESTIONS FOR FURTHER STUDY

Little research, if any, has focused on the relative importance
of the principal's socioeconomic status and race. Studies that

address this question could provide valuable information for researchers and practitioners. There is a debate in the literature on this issue and further evidence supporting the importance of one factor over the other would be useful in administrative training programs as well as in the placement of principals.

Several possible comparative studies could be done. A comparative study of African-American and white principals in less successful and more successful elementary schools could be done. The intent could be to examine the possible differences in leadership style associated with principal race and level of school success.

Other questions that could be pursued are: Is the leadership of African-American principals in more successful African-American elementary schools different from that of African-American principals in more successful predominantly white elementary schools? In more successful African-American high schools? In the first study, the possible effect of student race and/or socioeconomic status could be explored. In the second, the effects of the differences in high schools and elementary schools, which are said to have an impact on principal leadership, could be explored.

For purposes of narrowing my focus, I limited my respondents to teachers and principals. In subsequent research, parents, students, and central office staff could provide their perceptions of the principal's leadership.

In this study I also limited the number of variables affecting principal leadership. School socioeconomic status may be a major determinant of principal behavior. What researchers have previously perceived as characteristics of principals in more successful schools may be behaviors adapted to certain settings. This contention is supported by research which suggests that principals behave differently in schools with differing SES levels. Other factors that may affect principal leadership, according to some limited research, include grade level, staff size, district size, geographic location, and relative urbanization (Martinko and Gardner, 1983). Studies examining the impact of these variables on the leadership of principals are called for.

Finally, the situation that I observed at Collins is unusual in the literature and warrants further consideration. In fact, one teacher at that school said to me, "A more interesting study would be, in this school, why the scores go up and what the teachers are doing. I'm not sure it's the principal here." The way Mr. Charles' leadership, or lack of leadership, is expressed (i.e., through delegation to administrative staff and resource teachers) is worthy of further exploration.

In summary, suggested further research includes:

1. exploring the effect of the principal's socioeconomic status and race on leadership

2. comparing African-American and white principals in more successful and less successful elementary schools

3. comparing the leadership of African-American principals in more successful African-American schools with the leadership of African-American principals in more successful white schools

4. comparing the leadership of African-American principals in more successful African-American elementary schools and principals in more successful African-American high schools

5. replicating this study but including other respondents (e.g., parents, students, central office staff)

6. considering other factors as determinants of principal leadership (e.g., school socioeconomic status, grade level, staff size, district size, geographic location, and relative urbanization)

7. studying the leadership style exhibited by Mr. Charles at Collins

These questions and others warrant consideration as we explore further the link between principal leadership and academic achievement, in general, and the link between African-American principal leadership and African-American academic achievement, in particular.

REFERENCES

Beady, C. H., and S. Hansell. 1981. "Teacher race and expectation for student achievement." *American Educational Research Journal* 18, no. 2: 191–206.

Edmonds, R. 1979. "Effective schools for the urban poor." *Educational Leadership* 37: 15–24.

Kochman, T. 1981. *Black and White Styles in Conflict*. Chicago: University of Chicago Press.

MacLennan, B. W. 1975. "The personalities of group leaders: Implications for selecting and training." *International Journal of Group Therapy* 25, no. 2: 177–83.

Manasse, A. L. 1985. "Improving conditions for principal effectiveness: Policy implications of research." *Elementary School Journal* 85, no. 3: 439–63.

Martinko, W., and W. Gardner. 1983. "The behavior of high performing educational managers: An observational study." Working paper, Tallahassee: Florida State University.

Monteiro, T. 1977. "Ethnicity and the perceptions of principals." *Integrated Education* 15, no. 3: 15–16.

Morris, V. C., et al. 1981. *Discretionary Decision-Making in a Large Education Organization: A Report of a Research Project Funded by the National Institute of Education*. Chicago: College of Education, University of Illinois at Chicago Circle.

Peters, T. J., and R. H. Waterman, 1983. *In Search of Excellence: Lessons from America's Best-Run Companies*. New York: Warner.

Rist, R. 1970. "Student social class and teacher expectations: The self fulfiling prophecy in ghetto education." *Harvard Educational Review* 40, No. 3: 411–51.

Sarasan, S. 1971. *The Culture of the School and the Problem of Change*. Boston: Allyn and Bacon.

Wellisch, J. B., et al. 1978. "School management and organization in successful schools." *Sociology of Education* 51, no. 3: 211–26.

APPENDIX A: DEFINITIONS OF TERMS

African-American People   All people born, raised, and living in America who are descendants of African slaves.

African-American Schools   Elementary schools which have a student population that is two-thirds or more African-American.

Instructional Management   Primarily teacher supervision, achievement evaluation, and curriculum planning.

More Successful Schools   Schools that appear in the upper third of a rank ordering of the population of predominantly African-American elementary schools in California. The rank ordering is based upon a composite score for each school of the third and sixth grade math and reading scale scores on the California Assessment Program (CAP) Test for the years 1980–81 and 1981–82.

Principal   The chief administrative officer of a public elementary school. Excluded from this definition are superintendents who are responsible for individual school sites, vice or assistant principals, and any other school administrators not designated as a principal of a specific elementary school.

Principal Leadership   Developing goals, harnessing the energy of one's staff, facilitating two-way communication, and exercising instructional management.

APPENDIX B: TEACHER QUESTIONNAIRE

STANFORD UNIVERSITY
SCHOOL OF EDUCATION
PROGRAM IN ADMINISTRATION AND POLICY ANALYSIS
STANFORD, CALIFORNIA

STUDY OF BLACK PRINCIPAL LEADERSHIP AND ACADEMIC ACHIEVEMENT

The study is being conducted by Kofi Lomotey of Stanford University. The primary aim of this study is to learn more about the relationship between leadership of black principals and the academic achievement of black students in elementary schools.

All responses to questions are completely confidential. Completed questionnaires will be analyzed by Kofi Lomotey at Stanford University. Findings from this questionnaire will be reported statistically so that the identity of individuals will not be revealed. None of the questionnaires, once they are filled out and turned in, will ever be seen by anyone in your school.

I need the cooperation of many teachers like yourself, and the usefulness of my study will depend upon the sincerity and care with which you answer the questions. There are no right or wrong answers. My hope is that you will answer the questions in the way that you feel -- the way things appear to you personally.

INSTRUCTIONS

1. Please answer the questions in the order in which they appear.

2. Most of the questions can be answered by circling the number which corresponds to your answer. If you do not find the exact answer that fits your feelings, mark the one that comes closest to it.

3. Please answer all questions. The procedures to be used to analyze your responses require that all questions be answered in order for me to be able to use any of your responses.

4. Feel free to write in any explanations or comments you may have in the margins and on the back of the questionnaire.

5. Remember that the answers that you give will be completely confidential. It is important that you be as honest as you can in completing this questionnaire.

Part 1

The first part of this questionnaire is a series of yes/no questions for which you need only circle the correct answer, and scale questions for which you need only circle a number from 1 to 5, with 5 being the highest.

1. Academic Goal Formulation and Definition

    a. Does your school have goals?   yes   no

    b. How familiar are you with your school's goals?   1   2   3   4   5

2. Energy Harnessing

    a. Does your principal attempt to affect the behavior
        of staff members who may not be in line with
        the school's goals?   yes   no

    b. How effective would you say your principal has
        been in such situations?   1   2   3   4   5

158

APPENDIX B: (continued)

3. Communication Facilitation

   a. Does your principal attempt to communicate the school's goals to staff and students?　　　　yes　　　　no

   b. How effective would you say your principal has been in this communication?　　　1　2　3　4　5

   c. Do teachers in your school attempt to offer feedback on goals, school policies, etc.?　　　　yes　　　　no

   d. How effective are teachers in these attempts?　　　1　2　3　4　5

4. Instructional Management

   a. Do you view your principal as an instructional manager?　　　　yes　　　　no

   b. How would you rate your principal's instructional management skills?　　　1　2　3　4　5

Part 2

Please consider the on-the-job behavior of the principal of your school. Read each statement carefully. Circle the number that indicates the extent to which you feel he or she has demonstrated each behavior. If you feel unable to respond to a question because you do not know about a particular aspect of the principal's leadership, or if you feel that a particular question is not applicable, please circle the six (6).

1. ACADEMIC GOAL FORMULATION AND DEFINITION	Almost Never	Seldom	Some-times	Fre-quently	Almost Always	?
a. Frames the school's academic goals with target dates.	1	2	3	4	5	6
b. Frames the school's academic goals in terms of staff responsi-bilities for meeting them.	1	2	3	4	5	6
c. Develops academic goals that are easily translated into classroom objectives by teachers.	1	2	3	4	5	6
d. Develops goals that seek improve-ment over current levels of academic performance.	1	2	3	4	5	6
e. Uses data on student academic performance when developing the school's academic goals.	1	2	3	4	5	6
2. ENERGY HARNESSING						
a. Keeps staff working together as a team.	1	2	3	4	5	6
b. Has support of key teachers/ teacher groups.	1	2	3	4	5	6

159

APPENDIX B: (continued)

c. Distributes notes, announcements, or newsletters to teachers informing them of opportunities for professional development that are related to the school's goals.

    1   2   3   4   5   6

d. Selects in-service activities that are consistent with the school's academic goals.

    1   2   3   4   5   6

e. Distributes journal articles to teachers on a regular basis.

    1   2   3   4   5   6

f. Ensures that instructional aides receive appropriate training to help students meet instructional objectives.

    1   2   3   4   5   6

g. Arranges for outside speakers to make presentations on instructional issues at faculty meetings.

    1   2   3   4   5   6

h. Provides time to meet individually with teachers to discuss instructional issues.

    1   2   3   4   5   6

3. COMMUNICATION FACILITATION

a. Refers to school academic goals in informal settings with teachers.

    1   2   3   4   5   6

b. Refers to school academic goals at faculty meetings.

    1   2   3   4   5   6

c. Refers to school academic goals when making curricular decisions with teachers.

    1   2   3   4   5   6

d. Ensures that the school academic goals are reflected in highly visible displays in the school (e.g., posters and bulletin boards) indicating the importance of reading and/or math.

    1   2   3   4   5   6

e. Refers to school academic goals in assemblies.

    1   2   3   4   5   6

f. Keeps staff well informed.

    1   2   3   4   5   6

g. Is easy to understand.

    1   2   3   4   5   6

h. Is generally knowledgeable of staff personalities, problems, and interests.

    1   2   3   4   5   6

i. Uses needs assessment or other questionnaire to secure staff input on academic goal development.

    1   2   3   4   5   6

j. Finds time to listen to staff members.

    1   2   3   4   5   6

k. Looks out for personal welfare of individual staff members.

    1   2   3   4   5   6

APPENDIX B: (continued)

l. Is friendly and approachable.   1   2   3   4   5   6

m. Makes staff members feel at ease
    when talking to them.   1   2   3   4   5   6

4. INSTRUCTIONAL MANAGEMENT

a. Makes clear to teachers who is
    responsible for coordinating curriculum
    content across grade levels (e.g., the
    principal, the vice principal or a
    teacher).   1   2   3   4   5   6

b. Participates in meetings for the purpose
    of reviewing or selecting instructional
    materials.   1   2   3   4   5   6

c. Ensures that the academic goals of the
    school are translated into common
    curricular objectives.   1   2   3   4   5   6

d. Draws upon the results of schoolwide
    testing when making curricular decisions. 1   2   3   4   5   6

e. Ensures that the content selected from
    textbooks by teachers is aligned with
    the school's curricular goals.   1   2   3   4   5   6

f. Assesses agreement between school's
    curricular goals and the achievement
    test(s) used for program evaluation. 1   2   3   4   5   6

g. Meets individually with teachers to
    discuss pupil academic performance. 1   2   3   4   5   6

h. Discusses the item analysis of schoolwide
    tests such as the CAP with the faculty
    in order to identify strengths and
    weaknesses in the school's instructional
    program.   1   2   3   4   5   6

i. Uses the results of schoolwide testing
    to assess progress toward school
    academic goals.   1   2   3   4   5   6

j. Distributes the results of student
    testing to teachers in a timely fashion. 1   2   3   4   5   6

k. Informs teachers of the school's
    performance results on tests in written
    form (e.g., in memos or newsletters). 1   2   3   4   5   6

l. Informs students of the school's
    performance results.   1   2   3   4   5   6

m. Identifies students whose performance
    on school tests indicates the need for
    special instruction such as remediation
    or enrichment.   1   2   3   4   5   6

161

APPENDIX B: (continued)

4. INSTRUCTIONAL MANAGEMENT (CONT'D)

   n. Develops or finds the appropriate
       instructional program for students
       whose performance on tests indicates
       a need.   1   2   3   4   5   6

I appreciate the time and effort you have devoted to completing this questionnaire.

Thank you very much.

162

APPENDIX C: TEACHER INTERVIEW

The following questions were asked of the sample of teachers who were interviewed. As each interview developed, additional questions may have been asked, but at a minimum, these questions were asked.

1. GENERAL

   a. How would you rate the quality of the academic performance of the students in your school?

   b. Much of the literature on effective schools emphasizes the importance of the principal. What are your views on this observation?

2. GOAL DEVELOPMENT

   a. Do you have goals at your schools? (If no, skip to 3a)

   b. In what areas have goals been formulated (e.g., academics, climate, institutional)?

   c. What are these goals?

   d. Are these goals written?

   e. Do you have a copy of them?

   f. How were these goals formulated?

   g. Who was involved in their formulation?

   h. How effective have these goal formulation procedures been?

   i. What have been some of your school's less effective ways of dealing with goal formulation?

   j. In your view, how important are these goals in the daily operation of your school?

3. ENERGY HARNESSING

   a. To your knowledge, does your principal attempt to affect the behavior of staff members who are not necessarily in line with the school's goals? (If no, skip to 4a)

   b. In what ways does your principal approach such a situation?

   c. What have been some of your principal's most effective strategies?

   d. What have been some of your principal's least effective strategies?

4. COMMUNICATION FACILITATION

   a. Are you aware of any attempts by your principal to communicate the school's goals to staff and students? If yes, please describe these attempts.

   b. What have been some of your principal's most useful methods of communication?

163

APPENDIX C: (continued)

c. What have been some of your principal's least useful methods of communication?

d. Do teachers offer feedback on school policies, goals, etc.? (If no, skip to 5a)

e. What channels are used for this feedback?

f. Are teachers' channels effective?

g. Are teachers' channels sufficient?

5. INSTRUCTIONAL MANAGEMENT

a. What are the procedures for curriculum planning at your school?

b. Who is involved in these procedures?

c. How effective are these methods?

d. In your school, how is the evaluation of achievement handled?

e. Who is involved in this process?

f. How effective is this process?

APPENDIX D: COMPARISONS
OF FINDINGS OF
FOUR INSTRUMENTS

COLLINS	Goal Dvlpmnt	Energy Harnsg	Comm Facn	Curri Plan	Tchr Super	Achmt Eval
Teacher Questionnaire	NO	NO	NO	NO	--	NO
Teacher Interview	NO	NO	NO	NO	NO	NO
Principal Interview	NO	--	NO	--	--	--
Principal Observation	NO	NO	NO	--	NO	--
WOODSON						
Teacher Questionnaire	YES	YES	YES	YES	--	YES
Teacher Interview	YES	YES	YES	YES	--	YES
Principal Interview	YES	YES	YES	--	--	YES
Principal Observation	YES	--	YES	--	YES	YES
FOSTER						
Teacher Questionnaire	YES	YES	YES	YES	--	YES
Teacher Interview	YES	YES	YES	YES	YES	YES
Principal Interview	YES	YES	YES	YES	YES	YES
Principal Observation	--	YES	YES	YES	YES	--

Key:

NO =   data from instrument showed that principal did not provide direct leadership in this area

YES =   data from instrument showed that principal did provide direct leadership in this area

-- =   data from instrument was inconclusive or instrument was not used to measure variable

APPENDIX E: PRINCIPAL INTERVIEW

The following questions were asked of the principals in the sample. As each interview developed, additional questions may have been asked, but at a minimum, these questions were asked.

1. GENERAL

    a. How would you rate the quality of the academic performance of the students in your school?

    b. Much of the literature on effective schools emphasizes the importance of the principal. What are your views on this observation?

2. GOAL DEVELOPMENT

    a. Do you have goals at your schools?

    b. In what areas have goals been formulated (e.g., academics, climate, institutional)?

    c. What are these goals?

    d. Are these goals written?

    e. May I have a copy of them?

    f. How were they formulated?

    g. Who was involved in their formulation?

    h. How effective have your procedures for goal formulation been?

    i. What have been some of your school's less effective ways of dealing with goal formulation?

    j. How important are these goals in the daily operation of your school?

3. ENERGY HARNESSING

    a. Do you attempt to affect the behavior of staff members who are not necessarily in line with the school's goals?

    b. In what ways do you approach such a situation?

    c. What have been some of your most effective strategies?

    d. What have been some of your least effective strategies?

4. COMMUNICATION FACILITATION

    a. Do you attempt to communicate the school's goals to staff and students?

    b. How do you attempt this?

    c. What have been some of your most useful methods of communication?

    d. What have been some of your least useful methods of communication?

    e. Do teachers offer feedback on school policies, goals, etc.? (If no, skip to 5a)

    f. What channels are used for this feedback?

    g. Are teachers' channels sufficient?

    h. Are teachers' channels effective?

166

APPENDIX E: (continued)

5. INSTRUCTIONAL MANAGEMENT

    a. What are the procedures for curriculum planning at your school?

    b. Who is involved in these procedures?

    c. How effective are these methods?

    d. In your school, how is the evaluation of achievement handled?

    e. Who is involved in this process?

    f. How effective is this process?

APPENDIX F: CONSENT FORM

The purpose of this study is to improve upon the insufficient understanding of the effect of black principal leadership in black elementary schools in an attempt to ascertain similarities in the styles of several principals in selected more successful schools.

I understand the following:

_____ Principals only: I will be interviewed for approximately one hour. In addition, I will be observed for two full days in October 1984 and for two full days again in January 1985.

_____ Teachers only: I will be given a questionnaire to complete. Additionally, I may be one of five randomly selected teachers in my school who will be interviewed for approximately one hour.

My participation in this study is completely voluntary. I am free to withdraw my consent and discontinue my participation at any time, and I understand that my individual privacy will be maintained in the publication of any data resulting from the study.

I understand that if further information is needed by me, I may contact the researcher, whose name and telephone are listed below:

Kofi Lomotey

(415) 494-8623

If I have any questions or dissatisfaction with any aspect of this program, at any time, I may report grievances -- anonymously, if desired -- to the Human Subjects Coordinator, Sponsored Projects Office, Stanford, CA 94305 (or by phone [415] 497-3638).

_____
Signature of Subject

_____
Witness

_____
Date

APPENDIX G: KUMASI GREATER ACHIEVEMENT PROGRAM

FOSTER SCHOOL

RECORD OF CLASSROOM OBSERVATION

Teacher _____ Observer _____ Date _____

Grade Level _____   Time In _____ Time Out _____

Instruction Observed: _____ Reading   _____ Whole Group Others Present:

                                                                 _____ Two Group _____

                                _____ Direct   _____ Three Group _____

                                _____ Other (Describe) _____

Type of Instruction   Developmental
Observed: _____ Instruction   _____ Reteaching _____ Ext. Act

                                _____ Other (Describe) _____

SCHEDULE/PACING

                    Is the recommended pacing schedule being followed?   Y   N
                    If no, list the group(s) that are behind schedule.   __   __

                    _____

PRESENTATION OF LESSON

        The lesson: 1. was begun promptly   __ __
                        2. was appropriately paced   __ __
                        3. provided appropriate seatwork   __ __
                        4. included dist. guide and mater.   __ __

        The teacher: 1. stayed on task   __ __
                        2. involved all students   __ __
                        3. gave corrective feedback   __ __
                        4. gave clear directions   __ __

        Students: 1. stayed on task   __ __
                        2. involved all students   __ __
                        3. received immediate corrective feedback __ __
                        4. responded posit. to correct. feedback __ __
                        5. worked/completed seatwork   __ __

MANAGEMENT OF STUDENT BEHAVIOR

        Misbehavior and/or inattention was:

                        1. handled effect. and approp.   __ __
                        2. not observed   __ __

        Guidelines for personal and procedural needs of
        students were understood and followed   __ __

169

APPENDIX G: (continued)

CLASSROOM ORGANIZATION AND MANAGEMENT

The daily prog. and sched. of less. were posted   ___ ___
Minimal instructional time was used for classroom
management   ___ ___
Transitions were rapid and orderly   ___ ___
The teacher faced students being instructed and
could see the students doing seatwork   ___ ___
Students doing seatwork worked efficiently   ___ ___

SUMMARY AND RECOMMENDATIONS

Obser. strengths and/or sugg. for improve. of
instructional program _____

_____

1. obs. demo. lesson _____ 3. meet with CAP res. teacher ____
2. observe another teacher _____ 4. other _____

RECOMMENDED FOLLOW-UP COMMENTS: _____

_____

_____

Teacher's Signature   Date   Evaluee's Signature

APPENDIX H: PRINCIPAL PERSONAL DATA FORM

PERSONAL

Name: _____

           Last   First   Middle

School: _____

Age: _____ Marital Status: Married _____ Single _____ Other _____

EDUCATION

Highest Degree Held: _____ Total Number of Courses Taken in Education
Administration and/or Supervision _____

WORK EXPERIENCE

Teaching (in years)

Elementary _____ Area _____; Secondary _____ Area _____; Total _____

Administrative (in years)

Principal _____; Vice Principal _____ ; Other _____; Total _____

Other Than Education

Number of Years _____

Age When First Administrative Position was Held: _____

Total Number of Different Locations of Administrative Positions Held: _____

SCHOOL SITE

In what year was your school built? _____

What is the approximate percentage of each racial group in your school:

Black _____; White _____; Brown _____; Yellow _____; Red _____

Index

About the Author

KOFI LOMOTEY is Assistant Professor of Educational Administration at SUNY-Buffalo focusing on urban schools. He is currently working on three additional books: *Black Academic Achievement: What Black Educators Are Saying*, *The Urban School Principal: Facing the Future*, and *The Racial Crisis in American Higher Education: Problems and Solutions*.